ENDORSEM

"Government and Industry Executives, [...] with buying into a program based on advanced [...], data scientists, this book will be transformational for you and your program. It captures all the critical elements and decades of experiences into a few clear pages that will light the path for predictive improvements. I will be sharing it with my leadership and program managers. Great job, gentlemen, in making a complex equation simple to follow!"

—**Fred Walker**
Technical Director Counterintelligence, National Security Agency

"Amidst the concerns about the shortage of data scientists, a larger, overlooked obstacle is finding C-, VP-, and director-level leaders who understand enough about advanced analytics to hire, manage, and deploy solutions. Deal and Pilcher have written a practical and insightful 'primer for executives' to expertly fill this void."

—**Dean Abbott**
Co-Founder and Chief Data Scientist at SmarterHQ
Author of *Applied Predictive Analytics*

"Data science and big data often don't live up to their silver bullet hype. Why? Because IT and business are so different, and so hard to harmonize. This book is an excellent remedy; Deal and Pilcher distill a decade of analytics experience into a vital guide to what works. Mining Your Own Business is a must read for anyone interested in being right—by harnessing data to drive decisions."

—**Peter Aiken, PhD**
Founding Director/Data Blueprint
Associate Professor of Information Systems/Virginia Commonwealth University

"Deal and Pilcher have distilled their decades of experience into an easy-to-read book that will benefit any business person dealing with analytics. They keep technical details to a minimum while focusing on the key facts, decisions, and actions that business people need to be successful with analytics. Abundant real-world examples reinforce their practical and valuable advice. Your time reading the book will be well spent!"

—**Bill Franks**
Chief Analytics Officer, Teradata
Author of *Taming The Big Data Tidal Wave* and *The Analytics Revolution*

Mining Your Own Business

A Primer for Executives on Understanding and Employing Data Mining and Predictive Analytics

Jeff Deal & Gerhard Pilcher

Foreword by Eric Siegel

Data Science Publishing
Charlottesville, VA

Data Science Publishing
300 West Main Street, Suite 301
Charlottesville, VA 22903
www.MiningYourOwnBusiness.com
www.ElderResearch.com

Cover design and interior layout by Anita Jones, Another Jones Graphics

978-0-9967121-0-1 - print book
978-0-9967121-1-8 - ebook

Publisher's Cataloging-In-Publication Data
(Prepared by The Donohue Group, Inc.)

Names: Deal, Jeff. I Pilcher, Gerhard. I Siegel, Eric, 1968- writer of supplementary textual content.

Title: Mining your own business : a primer for executives on understanding and employing data mining and predictive analytics / Jeff Deal and Gerhard Pilcher ; foreword by Eric Siegel.

Description: Charlottesville, VA : Data Science Publishing, [2016] I Includes bibliographical references and index.

Identifiers: ISBN 978-0-9967121-0-1 (print) I ISBN 978-0-9967121-1-8 (ebook)

Subjects: LCSH: Data mining. I Business intelligence. I Business forecasting--Data processing. I Business--Decision making--Statistical methods.

Classification: LCC HD30.2 D43 2016 (print) I LCC HD30.2 (ebook) I DDC 658.4/038--dc23

Printed and bound in the United States of America

DEDICATION

To my parents, Tom and Anna Belle Deal,
for a lifetime of love, support, and encouragement.

—Jeff Deal

To Denise—my wife, best friend, great mom, and the one who
continues to make me feel like a love-struck 18-year-old.

—Gerhard Pilcher

We also dedicate this book to Dr. John Elder for encouraging us
to write it; for his red lined mark-ups on our previous articles
that continue to improve our writing; and for the courage to nurture
a company that values people, creativity, and high standards of
technical rigor and client service.

—Jeff and Gerhard

ACKNOWLEDGMENTS

Writing a book is, in at least one major respect, like conducting a successful data analytics initiative. Both require the contributions of a talented team. The team of dedicated people who helped us with this project is too large to mention by name, but we'd like to single out a few people for special recognition.

First, we want to express our appreciation to our Elder Research colleagues, whose insights, ideas, and encouragement have significantly enhanced this work. We would especially like to thank Dr. John Elder, the founder of Elder Research, for his invaluable contributions in content and editing, and Dr. Andrew Fast, Elder Research's chief scientist, for providing important technical material and carefully reviewing the manuscript. We're also much indebted to Parker Bleam and Todd Grabowsky for their help with the graphics.

We are very grateful for the many Elder Research clients who allowed us to share their stories in these pages. We'd especially like to thank Bryan Jones, who was formerly the deputy assistant inspector general for analytics for the U.S. Postal Service Office of Inspector General, and is now a member of the Elder Research team. Throughout the chapters of this book, he informatively shares his experiences as a champion of highly successful data analytics projects. His story is sure to inspire, encourage, and enlighten future champions.

We wish to thank the experts in the field of data analytics who took time out from their busy schedules to review the manuscript, especially Lewis Broome, CEO of Data Blueprint; Rafael Pabon, owner of Sherman Hill Group; and Yoony Doh, Advanced Analytics Practice Area Lead and Project Manager at Halfaker and Associates, LLC.

Michael J. Dowling of Wool Street Publishing, our talented professional ghostwriter and editor, expertly shepherded this book from conceptualization to publication. It was a pleasure to work with him as he magically transformed our technical expertise into understandable, polished prose.

A hearty "thank you" goes out to Sharon Castlen of Integrated Book Marketing for the outstanding marketing advice and book shepherding assistance she has provided to us. She really knows her trade! We also express our appreciation to Anita Jones of Another Jones Graphics, who did such a fine job laying out the book and designing its cover.

And finally, we wish to acknowledge the most important people of all: our wives and families. We truly valued their support and encouragement throughout this process of becoming first-time authors.

CONTENTS

FOREWORD

For predictive analytics to work, two different species must cooperate in harmony: the business leader and the quant. In order to function together, they each have to adapt. On the one hand, the quant needs to attain a business-oriented vantage. And on the other, the business leader must navigate a very alien world indeed. This book helps with that second bit.

Bridging this gargantuan divide is worth the effort. Take, for example, a tax fraud detection story worth ten digits (covered in the Introduction). Elder Research, Inc., the consultancy that spawned this book, delivered predictive models to the IRS that increased the agency's identification of a certain type of tax fraud by a factor of twenty-five. This saved the Feds billions (with a *b*).

This success exemplifies a widely applicable paradigm. Across commercial and government sectors, predictive targeting achieves a multiplicative improvement to broad scale operations (albeit often a single-digit multiplier rather than that whopping twenty-five-fold improvement). In addition to deciding which tax returns to audit, predictive models determine which customers to contact for marketing, which debtors to approve for increased credit limits, which patients to clinically screen, which employees to woo away from quitting, which persons of interest to investigate, and which equipment to inspect for impending failure.

Thus, data science earns its status as hot, lucrative, and sexy. This is the Information Age's latest evolutionary step, technology that taps data to drive decisions more effectively. It's the very act of scientifically optimizing resource allocation for…just about all processes. Various outlets have dubbed *data scientist* as the best, most in-demand, and even "sexiest" job. And if you haven't heard, data is the new oil. Industry research forecasts that demand will continue to grow and estimates the global predictive analytics market could reach as high as $9 billion by 2020.

To capture this value, you must construct a durable bridge across the quant/business culture gap. The core technology—which learns from data to predict—is only half of the trick. Deploying it is more than just a technical process—it's an organizational process. Existing business operations must change by way of implementing analytics. It's no longer business as usual; science now drives the enterprise's primary decisions and actions en masse. In this sense, data science is intrinsically revolutionary.

As a result, the greatest pitfall that hinders analytics is to not properly plan for its deployment. For each analytics initiative, it's critical to build a pathway from the get-go that will lead to integration. This requires bridging the cultural gap. It takes the socialization of buy-in: Line of business staff must agree to make big changes. To that end, they must learn what a predictive model does for them and they must be willing to put their faith in it.

That doesn't always work out. With refreshing frankness, this book reveals an Elder Research study of their own early client projects that showed a full third of projects fail to attain business results, despite 90 percent attaining technical (analytical) success. The difference is often whether the organization actually implements the fruits of analysis.

No guts, no glory. With inertia, resistance to change, and a lack of confidence as primary impediments, there's no more eye-catching antidote than Dr. John Elder's legendary willingness to put his money where his mouth is. Before founding Elder Research, John once invested all his own personal assets into his own predictive stock market trading system, in response to hesitancy on the part of his client to move forward (I recount this story in detail in the book *Predictive Analytics*). And in a story from Chapter 6 of this book, *Mining Your Own Business*, John doubled down against a major credit card company, betting Elder Research could beat their established analytical methods to model credit risk. If Elder Research failed, they'd cut their service fee in half, but if they won, the cost would double (yet, in the latter case, the company would gain enormously from the improved predictive model). This tactic served handily to move the project forward.

Don't worry. When inertia hinders progress, you don't necessarily need to take the dramatic approach of wagering your own money. There are other options among the established best practices for managing predictive analytics initiatives. It's largely about educating the organization and opening discussions to understand the concerns of skeptics.

Unfortunately, convolution and the appearance of arcane complexity threaten to extinguish a newcomer's excitement about the potential value. This might leave the person feeling compelled only by the pressure that comes from hype: "Everyone's doing it!" Let's nip that in the bud right now. Predictive analytics' value is simple and concrete: it helps run operations more effectively by way of predicting behavior, i.e., the outcome for each individual consumer, employee, healthcare patient, or suspect. These predictions are each just numbers, aka scores or probabilities. Since they directly drive decisions, by definition they are the most actionable deliverable you can get from analytics. One need only learn a limited bit about the (fascinating) "rocket science" that generates these predictive scores to integrate them and realize their value.

Regrettably, today's tremendous data hype does not always relay this value proposition or any specific value proposition at all. The pervasive buzzwords *big data* and *data science* enthusiastically remind us there is value to be had, but do not refer to any particular technology or approach. These terms are general catch-alls for "doing smart things with data." They really have no agreed upon definition beyond that, although they do allude to a vital cultural movement lead by thoughtful data wonks. *Big data* is nothing more than a grammatically incorrect way to say "a lot of data" (like saying "big water" instead of "a lot of water"). *Data science* is a redundant term, since all science involves data; it's like saying, "book librarian." In Chapter 2, the authors of this book delve deeper with solid coverage of the extensive taxonomy of terms and technology.

In a field propelled largely by data nerds, it may come as no surprise that most books serve the hands-on quant. Those books dive into the technical practice. After all, for a quant, the technology and software tools are much more tangible and easy to define than the more elusive, "human" arena of organizational processes and project management. As a natural-born geek, I know from personal experience.

This book is different. Jeff Deal and Gerhard Pilcher wrote it to serve the much neglected other side of the coin: you, the business leader. It delivers the two ingredients you need for success: 1) an understanding of the technology so you can speak the quant's language and 2) a guide to analytics management best practices, including how to build your analytics team and avert the most costly pitfalls.

In this book, the authors hand over an unmatched treasure trove of anecdotes accumulated at the firm from which they hail as executives—Elder Research, the most widely experienced data consultancy in North America. In contrast to vendors of analytics software, which traditionally are less likely to disclose the rough patches and challenges often experienced with analytics projects, Elder Research is an industry leader in deployment, across analytics software solutions and across sectors. The firm has accumulated a highly diverse portfolio of experience working with all major industry verticals as well as many government organizations, including defense, intelligence, and civil government.

With this book, Deal and Pilcher extend Elder Research's track record of thought leadership and industry education. This firm—and the two authors in particular—regularly contribute to the conference series I founded,

Predictive Analytics World. They head up two of its annual events, PAW for Government and PAW for Healthcare, and also provide various acclaimed presentations and training workshops at several other PAW events each year. If you have the opportunity to meet them in person, take it—but before you do, assimilate the wisdom they've labored to set forth in this book.

Eric Siegel, Ph.D., founder of Predictive Analytics World
and author of
Predictive Analytics: The Power to Predict Who Will Click, Buy, Lie, or Die
(revised and updated edition)

INTRODUCTION

Data mining and predictive analytics have been much in the news of late. In spite of all the hype—perhaps partly *because* of it—there's a lot of confusion about what these powerful decision-making tools are, how they function, and how they can best be utilized.

That's why we wrote this book. It's an easy-to-read, practical primer for C-level to mid-level executives about how to harness the power of these state-of-the-art technologies to increase organizational effectiveness. If you're a leader in an enterprise-level organization or a consultant to such organizations, you will find this book to be a useful introduction to the field and a valuable resource you'll refer to again and again.

When John Elder started our firm back in 1995, data analytics was in its infancy. We like to say that we were data scientists before it became cool. As early visionaries, we not only witnessed this revolution in management practice, we helped to create it. And we're still doing that today!

Over the past two decades, Elder Research, Inc. has served hundreds of clients in industry, government, and academia. We've acquired a wealth of information about what works and what doesn't, and in the pages of this book we share this inside knowledge with you. Below are some of the topics included:

- How to foster an analytic culture
- When and where data analytics can be most useful
- How the analytic process works from beginning to end (Hint: It involves more than analytics.)
- How to organize, staff, and manage data analytics initiatives
- How to build, implement, and evaluate data analytics models (an overview)
- When and how to hire analytics consultants
- How to approach the decision of what analytics software to purchase, if any
- How to avoid the most common data analytics mistakes
- How to integrate analytics into everyday workflows

Data analytics has been called the most powerful decision-making tool of the 21st century. Even though it has come of age only within the past twenty years, thousands of businesses, governmental agencies, and non-profit organizations have already used it to dramatically increase productivity, reduce waste and fraud, enhance quality, improve customer service, boost revenues, evaluate applicants, optimize strategies, combat crime and terror-ism, and solve a host of other tough challenges. Following are three actual cases from our company's files that help illustrate its value.

A worldwide provider of computer technology and consumer electronics knew that some service providers were submitting fraudulent claims and pocketing the reimbursements. This showed up in the simplest way, for example, when some of the same product serial numbers popped up again and again, but management did not know the extent of the problem, and they were oblivious to other more sophisticated scams. Our data scientists were able to discover several types of fraud schemes, determine the scope of the problems, identify the culprits, and develop corrective procedures. As a result, the company saved an estimated $20 million in the first six months of our consulting engagement and more than $75 million in the first five years.

○

The IRS needed to improve its models to identify fraud related to a type of tax refund. A serious data mining project by a team of companies over-hauled the data features and radically improved the model, which resulted in a 25-fold improvement in positive identification of fraud. The model and project are credited with saving over $7 billion in its first several years of use.

○

A regional provider of telecommunications services wanted to reduce "churn," which is the industry's term for customer account closures. Data mining work assisted management in determining the major causes of churn, and predictive analytics helped identify which customers were most likely to churn in the future. Developing solutions based on this data allowed the company to add approximately $1 million per year to its bottom line. In fact, these solutions currently generate more than enough savings each **month** *to pay for the* **entire** *multi-month consulting en-gagement.*

A management revolution is underway in the world of business and government. In the years ahead, the most successful organizations will be analytically competent. This book will help you gain the knowledge, vision, and passion you need to be on the cutting edge of this revolution.

HOW TO USE THIS BOOK

Mining Your Own Business provides an easy-to-read overview of data mining and predictive analytics for organizational leaders who want to know more about these powerful tools. It will also serve as a reference for those who want to develop an analytic capability in their organization.

Below is a summary outline of the book, with some suggestions about the level and type of leadership involvement required at each stage of the analytics process.

Establishing a Foundation and Vision for Analytics

This stage is critical to everything that follows. From the beginning, leaders need to invest enough time understanding the business and its mission, so they are able to identify and articulate to the organization the opportunities that analytics can address. They must prioritize goals and develop plans for the analytics initiatives, while taking into consideration the organization's constraints on funding, staffing, data availability, consultants, tools, and deployment.

See Chapters 4, 5, 6, and 12 for a discussion of these topics.

Fostering a Culture of Analytics

The extraordinary results produced by data analytics usually require the organization to undergo disruptive changes. Leaders must learn how to deal with the challenges of change, so they can successfully lead analytics initiatives with confidence, patience, and perseverance.

Managing change is discussed in some detail in Chapters 3 and 13.

Monitoring Analytic Projects

Early on, analytics leaders should devote considerable energy to understanding the business, defining the objectives of the initiative, and establishing measures of success. Once the data preparation and modeling begins, they need to monitor the progress of the project to ensure it meets the organization's objectives.

Leaders also must consider implementation of the model, because implementation constraints can impact the choice of modeling techniques and even precipitate disruptive changes to the organization's established business processes. Failure to initially budget sufficient finances and time for implementation can turn a valuable piece of software (the analytic model) into "shelfware" (a model unused by the business).

See Chapters 7, 8, and 12 for information on leading and monitoring analytics projects. Chapters 9 and 10 provide some technical details about modeling that will help leaders ask the right questions when hiring consultants and when assessing the quality and progress of projects.

Building Confidence in Analytic Results

It is the leader's responsibility to assess the process used to validate the model. An analytic model may be validated by asking the essential question, "Are the results it produces better than the results currently produced by other methods?" Sometimes the "other method" may be nothing more than "gut feel" or "educated guesstimates."

This topic is addressed in Chapter 11.

Putting Analytic Models into Operation

The leader plays a critical role in defining the business objective, which will drive the ultimate operationalization of the model. The many different implementation possibilities may range from simply running the model on an annual basis to creating a set of enterprise-level applications that incorporate analytic results into a business process. Outside consultants (if involved) typically pass the leadership role to the in-house team at the beginning of the implementation phase.

We address this topic in Chapter 12.

Additional Resources

We've listed some additional resources for further study on the book's website: *www.MiningYourOwnBusiness.com.*

CHAPTER 1

EMPOWERING THE DECISION MAKERS

The federal agency's Assistant Inspector General (AIG) seated across the table from us frowned as he scanned the report we had given him. He slid the document over to his second-in-command with a look that said, "You're not going to believe this!" Then he directed a penetrating gaze back at the two of us. "How did you know these things?" he demanded, slamming his fist on the table.

We were so startled that we instinctively reared back in our chairs and raised our hands, as if surrendering. "Don't arrest us," we blurted out. "No one gave us any inside information." Fortunately, our spontaneous reaction helped to diffuse the tension.

Six months had gone by since our initial sales presentation to this AIG. We had offered to give him a complimentary demonstration of the power of data analytics, but the data we needed to run our model had not yet been made available. So we decided to see what our proprietary predictive analytics software could do with data from public sources, such as the FPDS (Federal Procurement Data System). With the more limited data, our model operated at only about a third of its potential. Nevertheless, we were still able to predict with surprising accuracy which of this agency's contractors presented high risks of waste, fraud, and abuse.

Our preliminary demonstration of the power of data analytics created an "Aha!" for this AIG and his lieutenant. After things calmed down, they informed us that several contractors on the high-risk list we had given them were already under active investigation. In the past, this agency had typically relied on tips as the impetus for initiating investigations. They now saw how our analytics model could tell them not only which contractors to investigate, but where to start their investigations. This information would allow them to act instead of react, potentially saving their agency millions of dollars annually.

Hunting for Needles in Haystacks

Mining data for interesting and useful patterns is somewhat like looking for needles in haystacks. In this case, the haystack was composed of the approximately 50,000 contractors who did business with this federal agency. The needles were the contracts within this population that represented a high risk of fraud, waste, or abuse. Our approach was to remove as much "hay" as was practical; leaving the "needles" exposed and ranked according to degree of risk.

Rarely is it economically or technically feasible to remove all of the "hay." So, some of the contractors on our list were almost surely lower risk than thought, while others that weren't on our list probably should have been. However, by employing multiple analytical techniques, we pared down this large pool of contractors to a few hundred suspects, which we classified according to risk potential and major risk factors. Instead of spending valuable staff time inspecting a "haystack" of 50,000 contractors for a broad range of risks, the agency's inspectors could now focus their attention on specifically identified risks within a smaller pool of a few hundred suspects. This is just one example of the power of data analytics.

Breaking the Mind Barrier

The amount of information in the world is growing exponentially. The chart below illustrates some of the online information flow that now occurs every minute of every day, as well as the increase in Internet usage over a two-year period. Some types of data, such as thermostat readings or the monitoring of human vital signs in hospitals, are being created constantly!

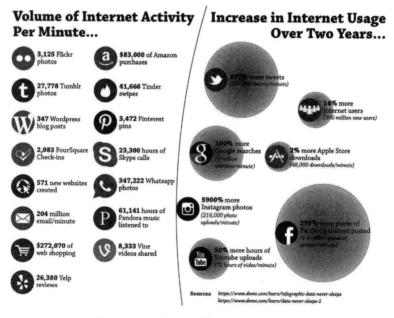

Figure 1-1: The Proliferation of Data

As the amount of information in the world increases, so does the amount of information that organizations must regularly scrutinize in order to make decisions. Humans are good at analyzing data, and computers will never take their place at the center of the decision-making process. However, research indicates that we humans can only hold five to ten pieces of information in our minds at one time. That's one reason why data mining and predictive analytics are so valuable. They filter and focus data, so we can better use our experience and intelligence to understand, interpret, and act on it. Data analytics does not replace human reasoning; it is an exponential multiplier of human reasoning.[1] Even IBM's Watson[2] can't match the human brain's ability to connect the context and semantics of information.

In his book *The Signal and the Noise*[3], Nate Silver talks about how human involvement can improve the results of analytical models. For example, studies have shown that the precipitation forecasts made by the National Weather Service's computer models are on average 25 percent more accurate when human weather experts interpret the outputs.

Computers are great at decision support when the decision parameters are known, but in real life, data can easily fall outside the programmed domain. For instance, when Captain Chesley B. "Sully" Sullenberger and First Officer Jeffrey Skiles called on their extensive flying expertise to safely crash land USAir Flight 1549 in the Hudson River on January 15, 2009, everyone on board was no doubt thankful that their lives were in the hands of real live pilots with the capability to creatively react to an extremely rare situation.

---

1   As our colleague John Elder likes to say, "Analytics doesn't replace a soldier with a robot; it puts the soldier in an Iron Man suit."

2   Watson is a question-answering (QA) computing system that IBM built to apply advanced natural language processing, information retrieval, knowledge representation, automated reasoning, and machine learning technologies to the field of open domain question answering. Watson is famous for winning $1 million on the TV quiz show "Jeopardy!"

3   Nate Silver, The Signal and the Noise: Why Predictions Fail—but Some Don't (New York: The Penguin Press, 2012), 125.

A World of Applications

All types of organizations are using data mining and predictive analytics to help them solve a wide range of problems. The following are a few examples from our client files of successful applications:

- Forecasting costs of long-term care for an insurance company
- Extracting relevant information from a large corpus of documents for a legal organization
- Predicting which natural gas wells will "freeze" and cease production for an energy company (allowing corrective action to save production)
- Evaluating grant proposals for likely success for a non-profit social welfare institution
- Assessing the causes of engine oil breakdown for a lubricant manufacturer
- Predicting the likelihood that students will accept offers of admission for a university
- Optimizing sales prices for an on-line retailer
- Analyzing reliability of satellites for a manufacturer of space products
- Projecting power utilization for an energy company
- Scoring loans for a banking institution
- Projecting crime location and timing for a law enforcement agency
- Evaluating patent infringements for a legal organization
- Detecting fraud for governmental agencies
- Predicting propensity to vote for a political campaign
- Assessing portfolio risk for a mortgage lender
- Predicting the likelihood of suicide for personnel at a governmental agency
- Analyzing the safety of airplane parts for a jet engine manufacturer
- Classifying employee satisfaction and drivers of employee turnover for a defense contractor

These are just a few of the many examples we could cite. The range of applications is practically endless. Data analytics is truly the most powerful decision-making tool of the 21st century!

Chapter Nuggets

- As the amount of information in the world increases, so does the amount of information that organizations must regularly scrutinize in order to make decisions.
- Data mining and predictive analytics help us filter data and focus it on key causes, so we can better use our experience and intelligence to understand, interpret, and act on it.
- Data analytics does not replace human reasoning; it powerfully leverages it.
- Data analytics is the most powerful new decision-making tool of the 21st century.

CHAPTER 2

CLEARING UP THE CONFUSION

Analytics and *reporting/analysis* are important decision-making tools. *Analytics* asks questions from data and gets answers, largely for predicting what is likely to happen. On the other hand, *reporting/analysis* describes what has happened in the past or what is happening in the present. In this book we will focus on the much more powerful decision-making tool of analytics.

It's easy to get confused by terms like *data mining, predictive analytics, data analytics,* and *big data*. This was certainly the case at one company we visited. "I'm going back to my office and do some data mining," we overheard a manager say. Later we noticed this manager sitting at her desk working on an Excel spreadsheet. We remarked to each other, "She's really going to be amazed when she sees the power of true data mining!"

This manager's misunderstanding was harmless. In fact, a spreadsheet was probably the best tool for her particular job, but she wasn't doing data mining. True data mining is the use of computers and advanced analytical algorithms to examine large amounts of data in order to discover meaningful patterns and insights.

In the data analytics field, different people and different organizations use some of the same terms in different ways. There is no consensus in the industry, and people frequently use terms interchangeably. Below are the meanings we'll use in this book for four of the most common terms.

Data mining is an inductive process that infers general patterns from specific instances (data), typically by machine learning. When properly applied, and when data exists to represent a wide enough collection of situations, the model can be even more powerful than those built by deductive methods, where expert knowledge is encoded. That's possible because inductive techniques can discover new rules or relationships previously unknown even to domain experts.

Predictive analytics is the use of a variety of techniques, ranging from statistics to data modeling to data mining, to analyze large sets of data and predict outcomes in order to facilitate decision-making. In his excellent book *Predictive Analytics: The Power to Predict Who Will Click, Buy, Lie or Die,* author and industry expert Eric Siegel defines predictive analytics as "technology that learns from experience (data) to predict the future behavior of individuals in order to drive better decisions."

Data analytics is a process of inspecting, cleaning, transforming, and modeling data with the goal of discovering useful information, suggesting conclusions, and supporting decision-making. Data mining and predictive analytics are two aspects of data analytics.

Big data is a very general term. Some people use it when referring to an amount of data that is too large to be processed using data analytics on a single computer. Others apply it to algorithms or techniques that are used to process data across distributed computers. And still others just use the term when referring to analytics in general. In this latter sense, *big data* is synonymous with the terms *data analytics, data science,* and *business analytics*.

Because of the dynamic nature of the industry, definitive definitions for these concepts are elusive. Nevertheless, we believe you will find these definitions helpful as you read this book.

Ten Levels of Analytics

Our colleagues, Andrew Fast and John Elder,[4] have created a helpful framework for understanding analytics. The ten levels they identify are listed below in order of increasing complexity. Higher levels often incorporate techniques from lower ones. Don't be concerned if many of these techniques are unfamiliar to you. We will discuss the most important ones in Chapter 6.

We've included questions and problems to illustrate how each level is used. Notice that the three data-driven levels (Levels 7-9) use the same example question. We employed redundancy to illustrate that although these levels differ in sophistication, they are interchangeable in their goals. In practice, there are few limits to the types of questions that models in these levels can address.

> **Level 1:** **Standard and Ad Hoc Reporting** produce reports from historical data, frequently by joining data from different database tables and/or by summarizing it by time periods or entities. For example, a report might join data from sales reports

---

4   This work by Fast and Elder first appeared in a white paper commissioned by the International Institute for Analytics.

for a specific region to data from employee records to show sales per sales rep for that region summarized by quarter.

- **Example Question:** How much did we sell last quarter by sales region?
- **Techniques:** Excel, SQL, OLAP

Level 2: **Statistical Analysis** uses *deterministic methods* (i.e., the application of formulae) to calculate statistical measures. Like Level 1, these measures look at the data historically, but they are more sophisticated than simple summarizations. They typically provide summary information about the data (e.g., average values, extremes, or standard deviations) and the strength of the relationship between two columns of data (correlations). Many of the most commonly known statistical measures are easily calculated using widely available software tools, such as MS Excel. Problems with poor characterization of data can arise, however, when these tools are used without a good understanding of underlying assumptions and adequate testing.

- **Example Questions:** What is the average dollar amount of an order for the month of April? Is the frequency of communication with customers correlated with satisfaction? (Note: A relationship between frequency of communication and satisfaction does not necessarily mean that frequency alone is causing satisfaction. Causation is a much more difficult question to answer than correlation. We will discuss this in Level 10.)
- **Techniques:** Means, standard deviations, correlations, principal component analysis (PCA), anomaly detection using Mahalanobis distance measure

Level 3: **Unsupervised Learning**[5] **(clustering)** employs algorithmic methods (i.e., methods that search or optimize based on the data, as opposed to deterministic methods based on formulae). It is used to explore relationships (groupings) among the observations (rows) in the data and relationships among

---

5   We will discuss supervised and unsupervised learning later in this chapter.

multiple features (columns), as well as to identify unusual observations.

- **Example Question:** What types of customers do I have? (By looking at historical data, one can segment customers and develop effective marketing approaches for each segment. When new customers arrive and provide data about themselves, they can be assigned to a segment based on the historical data. This data will then drive the type of marketing each new customer receives.)

- **Techniques:** K-means clustering, agglomerative models, anomaly detection using CADE method[6]

Level 4: **Business Rules and Alerts** use lower-level statistical techniques and known information about historical patterns to develop business rules and alerts to mimic these patterns as closely as possible. Subject-matter experts (SMEs) provide the historical information, ideally through a series of interviews designed to help reduce human bias.

- **Example Questions:** When do we notify a manager that the system load is dangerously high? Which contracts exhibit a greater risk of failure?

- **Techniques:** thresholds, such as JRules and Drools

Level 5: **Simulation** produces a range of expected outcomes based on thousands of iterations of calculations using a mixture of known and uncertain inputs. Statistical techniques (Level 2) can be used to measure and analyze the range of expected results.

- **Example Questions:** For a complex organization, what is the IT structure that will serve as the optimal call center? What is an acceptable response time for the help desk to return customer calls? What components of the help center have the biggest impact on responsiveness?

---

6 L. Friedland, A. Gentzel, and D. Jensen (2014) *Classifier-Adjusted Density Estimation for Anomaly Detection and One-Class Classification.* In Proceedings of the 2014 SIAM International Conference on Data Mining, Philadelphia, PA. pp. 578-586.

- **Techniques:** Monte Carlo simulation, stochastic modeling, agent-based modeling

Level 6: Optimization seeks to find the best (typically the most profitable or least costly) solution that is possible to achieve for a given set of resources and constraints.

- **Example Questions:** What number of investigators should we put on each case to maximize expected return? Where should a distribution center be located to minimize the time from order to fulfillment? Where should the center be located to minimize transportation costs? (Note: The different goals of the last two questions will likely result in different optimal locations. It might be useful to design a question that trades off several goals at once.)

- **Techniques:** integer and linear programming, local and global search

Level 7: Parameter Learning uses historical information about a known outcome to learn how to predict future outcomes, using a fixed set of selected inputs.

- **Example Questions:** How much additional cost do we expect this account to accrue in the next six months? Which contract opportunities have the highest win probability? Which employees are most likely to leave within the next year?

- **Techniques:** linear regression, logistic regression, neural networks, probabilistic graphical methods (PGM)

Level 8: Structure Learning discovers candidate model structures iteratively from historical data. Modern computing power and learning algorithms evaluate and select the best variables for a given model, and the best model(s) from a huge number of candidate model structures.

- **Example Questions:** How much additional cost do we expect this account to accrue within the next six months? Which contract opportunities have the highest win probability? Which employees are most likely to leave within the next year?

- **Techniques:** stepwise regression, decision trees, polynomial networks

Level 9: Ensembles[7] use a combination of discovered models joined together to improve the accuracy and reliability of predictions. Ensembles help overcome one of the potential pitfalls of single models (levels 7 or 8 above), which is that they can "over-learn" the historical data based on the known outcomes. Over-learning (or "over-fitting") results in less stable and less accurate predictions with new data. On the other hand, when multiple models are combined into an ensemble, each of the individual models contributes slightly different information to the prediction. The resulting predictions are generally much more stable, even if each individual model has over-learned the structure to some degree. Most importantly, they are usually more accurate than the component models.

- **Example Questions:** How much additional cost do we expect this account to accrue in the next six months? Which contract opportunities have the highest win probability? Which employees are most likely to leave within the next year?
- **Techniques:** random forests, bundling, bagging, boosting, Bayesian model averaging

Level 10: Causal Modeling, the cutting-edge frontier of analytic inquiry, blends expert assumptions and inductive learning to identify causal relationships from observational data. Its automated techniques are especially useful for aiding researchers and analysts when experimental data is difficult or impossible to acquire. For example, it would be unethical to run experiments on the effectiveness of new traffic legislation regarding seat belt usage, because it would require creating control groups in which some people were required to drive without their seat belts. Instead, modelers could use observational data (perhaps, in this case, National Transportation Safety Board accident reports) to identify possible "natural"

---

7   See Seni, Giovanni, and Elder, John. *Ensemble Methods in Data Mining: Improving Accuracy through Combining Predictions.* San Rafael, CA: Morgan & Claypool, 2010.

or "quasi-experimental" designs, such as comparing accident outcomes across states with different laws.

- **Example Questions:** How much of the reduction in fraud can be attributed to a change in investigative procedure? How do a state's tax laws affect its economy?
- **Techniques:** causal Bayesian networks, Rubin's Causal Model, quasi-experimental designs

Figure 2-1 summarizes the ten levels of analytics. The complexity of the models (as well as their power and potential danger for misuse) increases from the bottom to the top and from the left to the right.

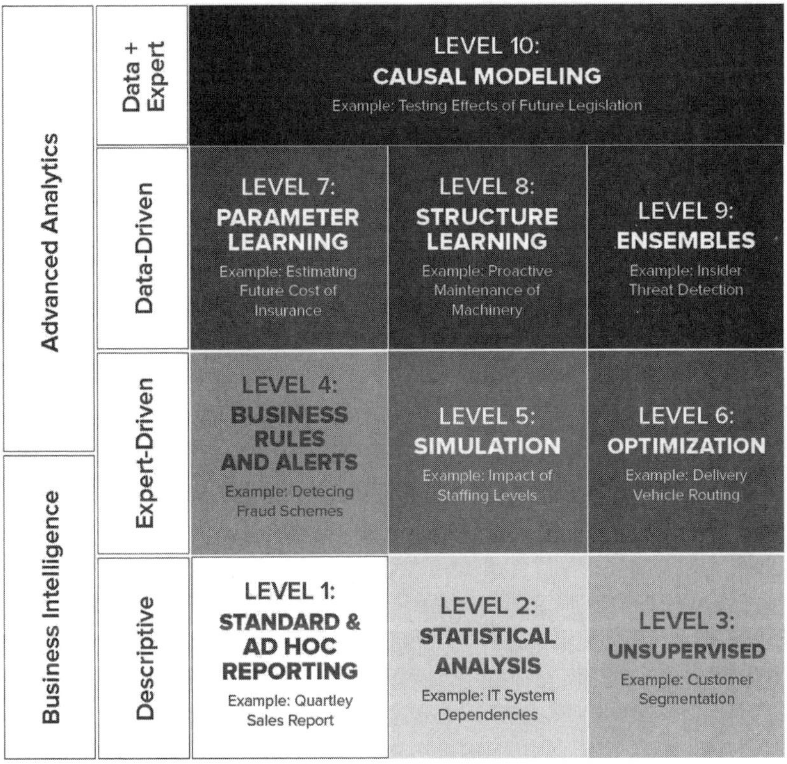

Advanced Analytics	**Data + Expert**	**LEVEL 10: CAUSAL MODELING** Example: Testing Effects of Future Legislation		
	Data-Driven	**LEVEL 7: PARAMETER LEARNING** Example: Estimating Future Cost of Insurance	**LEVEL 8: STRUCTURE LEARNING** Example: Proactive Maintenance of Machinery	**LEVEL 9: ENSEMBLES** Example: Insider Threat Detection
Business Intelligence	**Expert-Driven**	**LEVEL 4: BUSINESS RULES AND ALERTS** Example: Detecing Fraud Schemes	**LEVEL 5: SIMULATION** Example: Impact of Staffing Levels	**LEVEL 6: OPTIMIZATION** Example: Delivery Vehicle Routing
	Descriptive	**LEVEL 1: STANDARD & AD HOC REPORTING** Example: Quartley Sales Report	**LEVEL 2: STATISTICAL ANALYSIS** Example: IT System Dependencies	**LEVEL 3: UNSUPERVISED** Example: Customer Segmentation

Figure 2-1: Ten Levels of Analytics

Advanced analytics (Levels 4-10) can work with information from descriptive analytics (Levels 1-3), reconfiguring it to expose useful insights and facilitate decision-making. For example, by joining sales revenue data to sales activity data (e.g., numbers of sales calls, size of orders, time from initial sales call to closing of the sale, etc.), management can better determine what actions to take to improve performance.

We depict optimization as the most advanced form of the expert-driven techniques (Levels 4-6), because domain knowledge is essential to creating a useful simulation or an equation to optimize. Since most searches for parametric values are automated, we consider optimization to be a transitional form to the next higher levels of analytics (Levels 7-9) in the data-driven category.

The highest level, causal modeling, draws from both data-driven and expert-driven techniques. It functions like an automatic scientist who uses both theory and data to refine a hypothesis. Expert-driven modeling depends on the expert knowing the cause, and data-driven modeling can reveal a possible cause. However, only causal modeling can confirm a cause-and-effect relationship by combining both forms of knowledge to rule out alternatives.

Four Categories of Modeling Knowledge

All models combine knowledge from data with knowledge from human experts, both in the development of the model and in the actions taken based on the model outcome. For example, investigators provide information about credit card fraud schemes that have been investigated in the past, and data scientists build models to detect the schemes as transactions are processed. If the model detects a fraud scheme pattern, then the card may be automatically shut off from further approvals. Subsequently, humans can get involved (the cardholders and their banks) to resolve the disabled card. For example, was it truly fraud, or was it simply a set of unusual transactions by the card holder?

Both descriptive and predictive models have the potential to be *prescriptive,* which our colleagues, John Elder and Andrew Fast, define as *leading to an action without requiring human judgment.* Automatically shutting off access to a credit card is an example of prescriptive action.

Fast and Elder also define four categories for classifying modeling knowledge shown in Figure 2-2. As the figure shows, the two sources of knowledge—data or expert—are independent; a modeling technology can rely on either or both to a high or low degree.

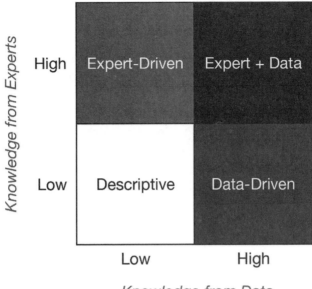

Figure 2-2: Data-Driven vs. Expert-Driven Knowledge

1. **Descriptive models** deterministically summarize data. They take aggregate data across potentially thousands, millions, and even billions of observations and systematically describe what has happened or what is happening in a form that humans can understand and use.
2. **Expert-Driven models** use computational methods to test expert opinions and assumptions. Expert-driven modeling is deductive; it reasons from theory to specific cases.
3. **Data-Driven models** induce new rules or formulas from data using automated search algorithms. Data-driven modeling is inductive; it reasons from specific cases (data) to a theory (model).
4. **Data+Expert models** combine deductive and inductive reasoning to determine causes from measured effects.

It's helpful to think about the balance between expert-driven and data-driven knowledge, both while planning for model development and while operationalizing the model. Expert-driven models require people who are subject-matter experts to participate strongly in the project. Because SMEs may come from other departments or organizations, it is critical prior to project initiation to plan for their input and gain commitment for their time. Naturally, understanding these concepts is important for budgeting and resource planning.

Data-driven models can require more automation development than expert-driven models to deploy, and they may potentially require more "marketing" to convince people to adopt them. For instance, models that are purely data-driven may not be directly interpretable, leading to the natural human response, "It can't be right if I don't understand it."

To help overcome this skepticism, at times we have run a complex, data-driven model in parallel with a simpler model. The people using the models gain trust in the data-driven model when they see that it consistently produces better results than the less complex model. Adequately planning for the balance between expert-driven and data-driven models increases project success.

Supervised vs. Unsupervised Learning

When we introduced the ten levels of analytics earlier, we called Level 3 "unsupervised learning," but exactly what is unsupervised learning? How does it differ from supervised learning, and why are these terms important?

Simply put, a model is unsupervised if there is no target or outcome variable. That is, a model to distinguish fraud from not-fraud is supervised, because it has a target variable (fraud), but an analytic project to find "what segments of customers exist" is unsupervised.

Operationally, the development of unsupervised models requires much greater input from human experts. The planners of the project need to provide adequate time and extra funds for collecting this input from the experts. Project planners should also realize that such experts will usually need to reprioritize their current tasks, so they will have time to provide their input.

The data associated with unsupervised models does not include historical outcomes as a key question of interest. Consequently, data scientists have fewer techniques at their disposal for building unsupervised models than they have for building supervised models. Since there are no known outcomes in the data when building unsupervised models, there is no way to directly compute the accuracy of these models. To develop a measure of the unsupervised model's predictive power, human experts must manually review a sample of model outcomes and tag the outcome as useful or not.

Now that you better appreciate the importance of understanding these terms, we will explain them in some detail using a simple illustration. Let's assume we want to build a model that will use certain variables, or inputs, to predict what grades students will earn. In the situation depicted in Figure 2-3[8], let's further assume that we have data that shows the grades that five students earned and the input variables relating to these students. Note that we have classified the input (independent) variables into two categories.

- *Treatments* are inputs that we can alter. In our example, they are the instructors, labs, and teaching assistants.
- *Covariates* are inputs we do not have the ability to change. In our example, they are the overall GPA, a student's gender, and a student's prerequisite grade.

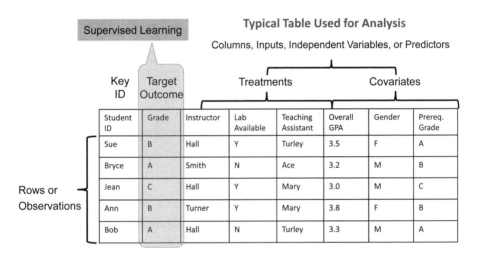

Figure 2-3: Supervised Learning

With this historical information, we can use *supervised learning* to build a model to predict the target outcomes (grades) for other students for whom we know the input (independent) variables.

If we do not know the target outcomes (grades) earned by the five students (see Figure 2-4), we might be able to group students into categories. That is, we might first use an unsupervised clustering algorithm to look for relationships in the data that naturally group students (a data-driven technique). Then we might look more closely at the characteristics of the groups that the clustering algorithm identified (an expert-driven technique), and we may even be able to label the groups in some way that

---

8 We wish to thank Mike Thurber, a lead data scientist at Elder Research, for providing Figures 2-3 and 2-4.

is helpful for knowing how to serve them (e.g., first-generation college, out-of-state, commuter, etc.).

To collect the information needed to make these predictions, we will interview subject-matter experts within the organization (e.g., teachers and administrators), examine records of previous experience, and employ other data-collection techniques. This model-building process is called *unsupervised learning*.

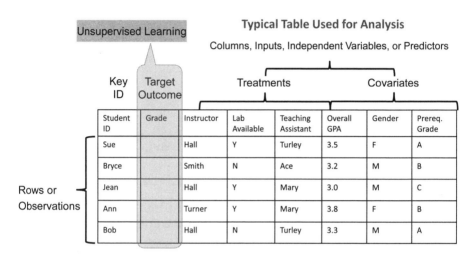

Figure 2-4: Unsupervised Learning

Unsupervised learning is technically more challenging than supervised learning, but in the real world of data analytics, it is very often the only option. For example, to create enough labeled cases when building a model to detect fraud, it's usually impractical to investigate (and thereby label) enough cases in a sample of data to see whether fraud exists. Without definitive historical information about target outcomes, the data scientist must use unsupervised learning techniques to build a model, and then look for anomalies (unusual cases) as a good place to start investigations.

Levels and Advanced Data Types

The examples and techniques described in this chapter focus on traditional, structured data. Yet the ten levels discussed previously apply equally well to advanced data types, including text, sequences, logs, time series, spatial, and multi-relational graph data. With graphs, for example, *link analysis* is a form of standard reporting, *social network analysis* is a form of statistical analysis, and *community detection* is a form of unsupervised learning. For more information on this subject, we refer you to the resources page of *www.MiningYourOwnBusiness.com.*

Because Levels 1 and 2 are well understood, this book will concern itself primarily with Levels 3-10. A considerable amount of misinformation and confusion attend these higher levels. Our goal in writing this book is to help clear away the fog, so you will be better able to define your organization's problems, assess the value that resides in your data, and determine which of your needs are best addressed by analytics. It has been our experience that data-driven modeling, simulation, optimization, and advanced analytics (Levels 5-10) offer organizations the greatest return on investment.

Chapter Nuggets

- *Data analytics, data mining,* and *predictive analytics* as commonly used are virtually synonymous terms. They refer to the process of inspecting, cleaning, transforming, and modeling data with the goal of discovering useful information, suggesting conclusions, and supporting decision making. These processes "learn" from experience (data) to predict the future behavior of individuals in order to drive better decisions.
- *Big data* is essentially *predictive analytics* on problems having a considerable flow of data.
- *Data analytics techniques* can be organized into ten levels, increasing in sophistication from various types of reporting to inductive and causal modeling.
- *Descriptive models* deterministically summarize data. That is, they aggregate data across potentially billions of observations and systematically describe what has happened in a format that humans can understand and use.
- *Predictive models* estimate what's about to happen (future unknown outcomes) by "learning" from historical data (past known outcomes).
- *Prescriptive models* lead to an action without requiring human judgment. Descriptive or predictive models may or may not be prescriptive (automatic).
- *Knowledge* can come from experts and/or be data-driven.
- *Supervised learning* has target or outcome variables. It uses known cases to find similar types of cases in future data.
- *Unsupervised learning,* where there is no target or outcome variable, is more technically challenging than supervised learning and requires more input from subject-matter experts.
- *Advanced analytics* (Levels 5-10) typically offer the greatest return on investment.

CHAPTER 3

LEADING A DATA ANALYTICS INITIATIVE

Leading a data analytics initiative is in some ways similar to gardening. Just as the first step in gardening is deciding what plants to grow, the first step with analytics is deciding what problems to solve. Begin by identifying a narrowly defined problem that is widely acknowledged within the organization as a pain point. One example might be customer or employee attrition.

As a data analytics goal, however, "reduce attrition" is overly broad. A better starting point might be "to identify characteristics associated with attrition." This more narrowly defined problem will be easier to solve, and it will still produce useful insights about attrition. A common misstep when first starting an analytics initiative is to take on more than the organization is capable of handling.

Organizations of any size have many problems data analytics can help solve. In picking your initial project, consider what problems keep you awake at night. What forces are impacting your organization that you need to understand better? What issues would you very much like to resolve? To ensure success, leaders should view the initiative as a vital step toward attaining the organization's overall goals. All involved in the project should buy into its success, and they should be willing to act on the insights the analytics will uncover. The project should be practical, with adequate funding and access to data. Especially at the beginning of the analytics initiative, it's essential to ask the right questions.

In the first chapter, we listed a range of problems our clients have addressed. Most of these types of projects could serve as a good starting place for your organization, as long as the scope is clearly defined. Some beginning projects that have worked well for our clients are reducing fraud, reducing customer turnover (churn), predicting costs, and improving production quality. Limit the focus of your effort. If your issue is fraud, for example, begin by identifying and reducing one particular type of fraud, rather than going after every form at once.

A primary purpose of your initial project should be to prove the value of data analytics and get people on board about its potential benefits. Obtaining buy-in is key, because analytics ultimately will change the way people in the organization make decisions. You must be prepared to lead change if you are going to thrive as an analytically-driven business. And to successfully lead change, you must gain commitment from the people who will be affected by producing useful results at an early stage.

View this initial data analytics project largely as a sales tool for future full-scale initiatives. Use it to demonstrate to all levels of management that the benefits of data analytics merit the required investment of time, money, and emotional energy.

Data analytics initiatives usually lead to significant changes in the organization's procedures and culture. Fundamentally, an analytic result should impact an organization's decision-making process. Most of us, at some point in our careers, have experienced difficulty implementing or adjusting to organizational change. There are many excellent books about leading change and overcoming human resistance to it, so we'll simply mention a few aspects specifically related to analytics.

For example, when implementing a model to reduce credit card fraud, consider the fundamental changes that have to be put into operation in order to process credit card transactions differently. The system has to score hundreds of millions of transactions per day and keep a record of recent, related transactions. When a transaction exceeds established risk thresholds, the system must automatically suspend approvals. And even before the system can become operational, the credit card company has to retrain all call center attendants and provide them with a set of tools to assist owners of suspended credit cards.

Changes such as these can be uncomfortable, and they are often controversial. That's why it's crucial to sell the benefits of data analytics and gain buy-in during the early stages of the project.

Occasionally an organization with no specific purpose in mind asks us to come in and help it build a predictive analytics model. The executives assume we can provide a magical "black box." They expect us to dump their data into it, turn the crank, and generate insights that will enable them to transform the way they run their business. Occasionally we can produce some extraordinary results from that sort of non-directed approach, but we strongly discourage it.

If there are no burning issues keeping people in your organization awake at night, and if no one is asking for the results you'll create, the project will probably turn out to be a waste of time and money. That's exactly what happened with one large government contractor who hired us to build the organization's analytics capability.

When we asked the senior executive of this organization how he intended to use the insights the model would produce, he said he didn't know, but that he was confident several units in the organization would find the information useful. We cautioned him against imposing a project from the top down, and we urged him to find a sponsor or client within the organization who wanted a particular problem solved. We went on to explain that committed stakeholders are much more willing to contribute to the project by providing subject-matter experts and cooperating in other ways.

Unfortunately, this executive insisted on proceeding with his "if we build it, they will come" approach, and our fears materialized. Even though the model we built produced good results, no one within the organization was interested in them. For its considerable investment of time and money, this client merely ended up with a solution in search of a problem.

Starting Small

Some companies new to data analytics try to push ahead too fast. Instead of investing $75,000 or so in a modest initial project, they rush out and hire two or three people who have some experience with analytics, spend $500,000 on software, and announce that the company is now "data-driven." However, pursuing a data analytics initiative without proper planning and organizational buy-in is like purchasing an expensive piece of home exercise equipment without sufficient commitment. The equipment may seem exciting at first, but without a dedicated regimen, it will soon end up sitting idle in the basement or serving as a clothes rack in the corner of the bedroom.

Several years ago the managers of a very large company asked us to help them with their vision for using data analytics as a vehicle for transforming the entire healthcare industry. After our team of four people met with their team of twelve people for two days, it was clear that the organization's vision was too grandiose to get off the ground. It was as if they were trying to reach the moon with a hobbyist's model rocket. After two days of meetings, the potential project collapsed under the weight of its unrealistic goals.

In contrast, another of our clients, one of the largest insurance companies in the United States, did everything correctly. When we came in for the initial kickoff meeting, the leader of the project had already assembled the key SMEs, executives, IT people, and other stakeholders. The project this company presented to us involved a widely acknowledged, well-defined pain point associated with a particular line of insurance. Its clear focus and narrow scope led to highly productive meetings and substantial buy-in.

Although committing all of these people to a day and a half of meetings was expensive, the investment paid off. The initial project was very successful, and since then the company has applied data analytics to other problems associated with this same type of insurance. In the future, they plan to expand data analytics into other lines of their business.

Something else impressed us about this client. We were delighted to find that the person responsible for data security was very forward-thinking. She was determined to do everything possible within the law to make the information our initiative required available. In our experience, far too many data security people are afraid to share any information that contains personal data about customers or clients. Fortunately, this person put forth the extra effort to get us the data we needed, without violating customer confidentiality or the law.

Examples of Poor vs. Good Focus

Let's discuss two cases that demonstrate the importance of focus. The first involves a national lending organization that asked us to create an analytic model for identifying high-risk loans. The firm operated in most of the fifty states, and each state had different types of data, different methods of storing data, and different laws pertaining to the lending business. The company wanted one model for all states that would score potential borrowers on their likelihood of defaulting on their loans.

Although the overall goal was reasonable, we immediately saw that the company would need almost fifty different models. Unfortunately, when we told management that individual models would be needed for each state, they did not take our advice. Due to this and other organizational problems, the project never got off of the ground.

A more positive outcome resulted when a prestigious post-graduate school at a large university asked us to help them identify which applicants were likely to accept an offer of admission, if extended. The school provided us with several years of applicant data that had been scrubbed of personal identifying information. It included all of the information pertinent to the admission decision, such as the name of the undergraduate college the applicant had attended, the applicant's major as an undergraduate, and the amount of financial assistance the institution was offering the applicant.

For the training data, we also knew the outcomes (i.e., which applicants had received offers of admission, and which offers had been accepted).

The university decided to focus the model on a very simple question: "If we make an offer of admission to a student, what is the probability that this student will accept the offer?" We could have built a model that would answer other questions as well, such as, "If we admit a certain applicant, what is the probability that this applicant will eventually graduate?" Or, "If we admit a certain student, into what quadrant will this student likely fall in the class rankings?" To their credit, the school resisted the temptation to broaden the initial focus. Their narrowly defined target made each aspect of the work easier and more efficient. This project was a big success and a pleasure to conduct.

Cultivating the Culture

Returning to our gardening analogy, after deciding what to plant, the next step is to cultivate the soil. Similarly, the second step in data analytics is to cultivate the organizational culture. This entails developing the analytic plan, setting goals, and gaining buy-in from the people who will be involved.

Because a data analytics initiative will draw on knowledge, services, and resources from multiple areas, commitment to it must be broadly shared within the organization. All participants need to view the project as an important component of the company's vision. A project with a weak commitment will likely wither and die.

A predictive analytics project we conducted for a major government agency revealed that the satisfaction of customers increased when response times to their complaints decreased. This insight surprised no one, but the project did arouse attention when it identified a point beyond which further reductions in response times were not worth the cost. In other words, the agency's customers weren't noticeably happier when the customer service response times were cut from forty-eight hours to twenty-four hours. Based on this analysis, we demonstrated that responding less quickly could save the agency about $2 million dollars per year, without any significant loss in customer satisfaction.

Unfortunately, more than two years have passed, and this agency has yet to optimize its response times in accordance with our recommendation. We're always disappointed when we see a predictive analytics program with a large potential benefit discontinued in midstream, but it happens quite a lot. As with most other significant organizational changes, implementation of data analytics recommendations will usually require adjustments to the company's culture and processes. These changes are never easy, and sometimes implementation is further hindered by corporate politics or bureaucratic inflexibility.

In contrast, the leaders of another organization we worked with did an especially fine job of laying the groundwork for cultural transformation. One of their key moves was to ask a few potential users of the results to serve on the initial installation team as subject-matter experts for their particular areas of responsibility. Although these individuals were not data-driven people by nature, their exposure to the data analytics process turned them into believers. When they saw the potential benefits that the data-driven models would produce in their own areas, they became very effective cheerleaders. Other potential users of data in the organization jumped on board. Soon, virtually everyone had bought into the initiative.

Managing a Data Analytics Initiative

With a data analytics program, a small success serves as the foundation for greater success. As with a garden, long-term success takes commitment, patience, and on-going tending. Just as a gardener must water and fertilize the garden until the plants appear, the leaders of a data analytics initiative must provide encouragement and guidance until the insights surface and appropriate actions are undertaken. And just as a gardener must pull weeds that would crowd out the plants, the leaders of a data analytics initiative must guard against distractions that would undermine the project's success.

Because the results of a data analytics project can take quite some time to manifest, staying the course can require considerable patience and perseverance. As an organization continues to invest time and money into the initiative, some leaders may get anxious or even fearful. "What if this project doesn't pan out?" they may start thinking. "Are we simply pouring money down the drain?"

Sometimes other people will suggest other problem-solving techniques, and leaders may be tempted to divert funds from the data analytics initiative to alternative approaches that may appear to be faster and cheaper. Leaders should continually remind themselves and all involved that quick fixes rarely provide effective long-term solutions to complex problems. Courageous, positive leadership is necessary to ensure that the data analytics initiative stays on course until successes begin to manifest. At the same time, the analysts need to keep those working on the initiative encouraged with reports of early findings.

The Experiences of a Mobile Phone Service Provider

The management of a regional provider of mobile phone services asked us to build an analytics model to predict which of their customers were most likely to "churn" (i.e., switch to a competing carrier). Our client planned to give these predictions to call-center operators, who would then telephone these high-risk customers prior to contract expiration and explain the advantages of renewing their current contract.

We had confidence in the model we built, but its results, during the first several weeks of operation, were disappointing. Even though call-center operators were telephoning the customers we had identified as high risk to try to persuade them to extend their contracts, churn remained high. Management wondered if their rather significant investment in predictive analytics had been a mistake. Even we were starting to feel perplexed!

Upon further investigation, however, we discovered that the model was working fine. The problem was with the scripts that call-center operators used when making calls. It turned out that when operators were unable to reach the customers identified as high risk, they were leaving voicemail messages that their service contracts were about to expire. These messages had the unintended negative effect of alerting these customers that they would soon be free to change carriers without penalty. This resulted in more churn, not less, because these calls essentially prompted customers to change carriers when they otherwise might not have thought about it. As the saying goes, it would have been better if the call-center operators had "let sleeping dogs lie." Our discovery about how call-center procedures were actually promoting churn created the first of a series of "aha moments" for the company.

When management told operators to forego voicemail messages, churn decreased dramatically. A comparison of the actions of potential churners who received a phone sales pitch to the actions of a control group that did not have the benefit of the sales pitch showed that our initiative was saving the company more than 200 customers per month. This quantitative evidence of the value of predictive analytics created the second "aha moment" for the client. These results were especially gratifying to our client, because at this time, the company was operating at a competitive disadvantage in the marketplace. The newly released iPhone was dominating the market, and at that time our client was not authorized to sell it.

A few months later, when the company became an authorized distributor of Apple products, management decided to deemphasize this initiative. They figured that churn wouldn't be an issue, because customers no longer had to go to a competitor to buy the iPhone. Under pressure to divert some of the data analytics resources to other initiatives, management cut the call-center support for the analytics campaign by two-thirds.

The results were disastrous. The company's overall churn increased dramatically, so that our campaign was now preventing zero churns per month. When management reestablished the analytics initiative to full strength, churn savings shot up past 200 to more than 500 customers per month. This third "aha moment" convinced the client of the value of predictive analytics.

Figure 3-1 illustrates the costs and benefits of the first ten months of this program. The solid line depicts the company's cumulative investment in the project, and the dotted line represents the cumulative additional revenues produced by the initiative. Note that management had to invest funds into the project for four months before any new revenues began to materialize. As we have said, leaders must exercise patience, perseverance, and sometimes even courage while waiting for results of data analytics initiatives to manifest.

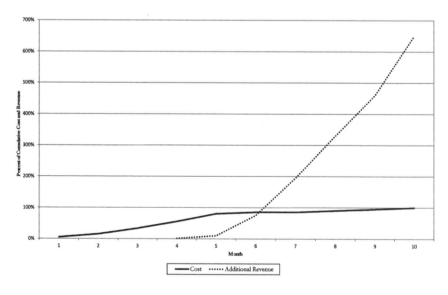

Figure 3-1: Cumulative Percentage of Cost and Revenue

This client did not give up, and in the fifth month the payoff started to appear. Initially, the return on investment was small, for reasons explained above. After the company modified its call-center procedures and added the iPhone to its product line, the additional savings produced by the model accelerated rapidly. At month six, the company reached a breakeven point, where the cumulative additional revenue generated by the initiative had fully offset the cumulative amount invested in the project.

By this time, the company had invested about 95 percent of the total amount of funds that would be required, and the additional cumulative revenues were rising rapidly. By month ten, the additional revenues produced by the model were 6½ times greater than the cumulative cost of the project. On an annual basis, the return on investment was above 750 percent and still rising! In fact, with each passing month, the business generated enough additional savings to pay for the entire cost of the investment in analytics. Today the company continues to reap substantial benefits from this model, and it is expanding the application of analytics to other areas of its business.

BRYAN'S STORY
Part 1: Launching a Data Analytics Initiative

Starting in this chapter, Bryan Jones will share his experiences as the leader of a successful data analytics project. We will include additional installments of his story in subsequent chapters. At the time of this project, Bryan was deputy assistant inspector general for analytics for the U.S. Postal Service Office of Inspector General. Here is the first installment of his experience in his words.

I'm somewhat surprised that I got involved with analytics in the first place. I was never good at math, and it took me two years to get through Algebra II. But I could translate data into terms that business people understood and found useful.

I believe my success as a leader of data analytics projects was due largely to the business and personal relationships I had built over eight or nine years with the inspector general and with a lot of the directors, managers, and staff. Even if people didn't understand analytics or care a lot about it, they would listen to me and give me the benefit of the doubt, because of the strength of our relationship and the credibility I had earned with them.

I would say something like, "You guys are the experts. If you give us a good problem to solve and send us somebody to work on it, we'll try to put something together. When we're done, you can tell us if it's valuable." I knew from my background as an auditor that we had a good product. My sincere desire was to help others see its value and benefit from it.

Leadership is Key

A study our firm conducted of the projects we had completed in our first decade since our founding in 1995 showed that 90+ percent had been technical successes, but only 65 percent of those had been implemented; that is, only two-thirds had been business successes.[9] Many causes can contribute to a lower business success rate, but the biggest one is a lack of organizational commitment to implementation. Unfortunately, many organizations simply are not willing to operationalize the recommendations that the analytical work provides, even when it's obvious that these recommendations will lead to significant improvements.

Why do so many organizations invest significant amounts of time and money in a data analytics project and then fail to implement the resulting recommendations? By this stage, they've paid all the costs, and they have proven returns on out-of-sample data. Without implementation, however, they realize no gain.

We believe the two major reasons are the absence of strong leadership and a lack of buy-in by key decision makers. (A minor reason is failure to understand the results, which is a failure on the part of both analyst and client.) To implement data analytics recommendations, organizations often must develop new policies and procedures, change long-standing processes, retrain personnel, and even transform corporate cultures.

Increase the probability of success by involving key stakeholders from the beginning. A data analytics project is likely to fail if you conduct it without involving the stakeholders, and then upon completion tell them, "Here's what the data shows. Now make use of it."

Changing a corporate culture is never easy. That's why successful predictive analytics initiatives demand strong leadership from one or more "champions" who are enthusiastically committed to analytics and who command sufficient respect within the organization to enlist the commitment of others. We'll close this chapter by relating a few stories about what has worked well and not so well with some of our clients.

---

9   Studying our past – data mining our data mining – proved very fruitful. By identifying the major non-technical obstacles to putting a new model and process into production, we were able to avoid most roadblocks in the future and get our production rates up substantially in the following decade.

A Parade of Champions at a Federal Agency

In a successful project we conducted for one of the larger federal oversight agencies, the head of the agency was the visionary champion. He established the cultural expectation that the organization would become data-driven, and he used his budget authority to make sure the funds would be available to pay for the necessary consultants, software, and internal services.

A short time later, another champion who was quite analytics-minded arose from a lower level of the organizational ladder. He identified a specific problem that needed to be solved and helped to convince people that data analytics was the best approach. About two years later, a third champion emerged. This key person, a very practical leader, became the quarterback and cheerleader who led the first project to successful completion. Each champion was able to build on the momentum and foresight of the previous one. Because all three operated at different levels in the organization, they could communicate strategically or tactically as that level demanded.

A Lack of Leadership at a Financial Firm

Another case from our files didn't turn out so well. After a preliminary analysis of data, we submitted a proposal to a Fortune 500 financial firm that showed that for an investment in data analytics of about $500,000, this firm could reduce its overseas workforce by about 75 percent. This promised to save tens of millions of dollars annually, with no adverse effects on operational effectiveness. Management could allow these savings to flow through to the bottom line, or perhaps even better, they could use them to train the company's foreign workforce to collect and verify data needed for new products it wanted to offer.

Three years have now passed, and the company has failed to act on this recommendation. Why? It's not an issue of money. Yes, $500,000 is a significant investment, but the potential return on this investment is huge. Technical issues aren't the problem either. Management knows that predictive analytics is a proven science, and they agree that the preliminary study was a big success.

The fundamental problem is lack of leadership. Management started off on the wrong foot by failing to involve key stakeholders. This led to less than optimal buy-in. When the project got underway, various departments dug in their heels. The company's IT department, for example, viewed the initiative as a threat. They were afraid it would take work away from them and possibly make them look bad. Along with other units in the organization who had similar feelings, they sold management on the idea of doing the project internally. Since the company lacks the analytics capability to do the job right, to this day the work remains unfinished and ineffective, and the savings remain unrealized. This type of corporate paralysis is not unusual, especially when the decision involves many different stakeholders within an organization.

The Effect of Different Leadership Styles at a Government Agency

Another government agency we have worked with has had very good success with predictive analytics in one area of the organization and much less success in another. The difference is due almost entirely to the leadership styles of the key people involved. In the first case, the key person is a true champion of data analytics. He believes in its potential, and he's very willing to implement the recommendations it produces. In the other case, the key person is extremely cautious about data analytics and hesitant to act on the insights it generates. He sees it more as a drain on resources than as a generator of value. Unfortunately, this mindset has turned out to be a self-fulfilling prophesy.

Bold Leadership Required

The insights produced by a predictive analytics process are worthless unless acted upon. Unfortunately, many organizations lack the courage and determination to implement the resulting recommendations, especially when they run counter to conventional wisdom, or when they demand substantial changes to long-standing procedures. We humans are more strongly influenced by our biases than we generally realize. Learning to trust and utilize data instead of relying on past experience and "gut feel" can be as challenging to business leaders as learning to fly an airplane by instruments rather than by sight can be to beginning pilots.

The difficulty of implementing analytics recommendations is captured in the fascinating book (and movie) *Moneyball*, which describes how Billy Beane, the general manager of the Oakland Athletics, had to battle seasoned baseball veterans and long-standing baseball traditions in order to install a data capability for his team. Even his own team manager resisted his efforts. To champion this transformation, Beane had to be the visionary, cheerleader, encourager, teacher, cajoler, and drill sergeant—essentially, he had to play every role except that of the analytic model builder. Such leadership is demanding and often lonely, but in this case Beane successfully transformed the culture and made a good baseball team a whole lot better, ultimately generating a huge reward. He serves as an excellent role model for aspiring leaders of analytics initiatives.

Chapter Nuggets

- Most organizations, of any size, have problems data analytics can help solve.
- In picking your initial project, consider what problems keep you awake at night.
- Obtaining buy-in from fellow stakeholders is key because analytics ultimately will change the way people in the organization make decisions.
- Data analytics initiatives usually lead to significant changes in the organization's procedures and culture. These changes can be uncomfortable or even controversial, so it's crucial to sell the benefits of data analytics and gain buy-in early on.
- Because a data analytics initiative will typically draw on knowledge, services, and resources from multiple areas, commitment to it must be broadly shared within the organization.
- With a data analytics program, a small initial success serves as the foundation for greater success.
- Because changing a corporate culture is never easy, successful predictive analytics initiatives demand strong leadership from champions who are enthusiastically committed to analytics and who command sufficient respect within the organization to enlist the commitment of others.
- The insights produced by a predictive analytics process are worthless unless acted upon. Unfortunately, many organizations lack the courage and determination to implement the resulting recommendations, especially when they run counter to conventional wisdom, or when they demand substantial changes to long-standing procedures.

CHAPTER 4

STAFFING A DATA ANALYTICS PROJECT

We recently noticed a recruitment ad for a data scientist that listed the following required skills:

- 5 years of experience in data mining and media or advertising analytics
- Proficient in at least two programming/scripting languages: Python, Ruby, Pig, Java, Hive, PHP, JS
- Specific experience using tools such as Mahout, Hadoop, Cassandra, Splunk
- Hands-on knowledge of database manipulation through environments such as MySQL, NoSQL
- Experience working with Linux/Unix platform Facile with statistical computing using R, SAS, SPSS, or S-Plus Skilled in K-Means and K-means clustering, MapReduce
- Ability to decompose a problem and work through a technical approach and attack a problem in a systematic way
- Solid experience with machine learning and data mining
- Experience with digital metrics systems such as Adobe Site Catalyst or Google Analytics Premium
- Experience with Google Analytics API
- Strong analysis and experimental design skills with a keen sense for data gaps and inconsistencies
- Experience in developing data visualization independently or with tools such as Tableau
- Excellent oral, written and visual communication skills, particularly at explaining complex quantitative information to non-technical audiences
- Strong collaboration skills
- Not just a tolerance but a zeal for multitasking. At the same time show a clear sense for priorities and commitment to follow-through
- Experience managing data-driven research from project inception to client communication
- Ability to work independently with little supervision as well as in collaborative team environment
- Self-starter with the ability to work in a constantly changing environment

Whew! This company will need to look for a long, long time before it finds someone with this array of talents. In fact, they may never find one of these "super scientists."

Individual or Team?

Data science is a highly complex discipline demanding diverse skills. Every data analytics initiative requires proficiency in statistics, machine learning, algorithms, hacking, databases, and industry/domain knowledge. In addition, each initiative needs a person or persons capable of managing projects, interfacing on a business level with top managers, manipulating data, and handling a host of other responsibilities. Is it possible to find a data scientist with all of the needed skills, or are these various roles best filled by a team?

That's essentially the question Gregory Piatetsky[10], president of the consulting firm KDnuggets, recently posed in his highly respected blog[11]. More than 300 industry experts responded, and their opinions were about evenly divided. Although there seems to be no consensus about whether the individual or team approach is better, experience has led our firm to favor the latter.

A team building a predictive model typically consists of people with the following backgrounds and talents:

Data expertise:

- One or more **data scientists** who will build the model using their specific expertise
- One or more **data software engineers** who will create the software around the analytic model
- One or more **data wranglers** who will construct and maintain the analytics base tables (ABT), which transform the client's data into a form that is more suitable for modeling

---

10 Gregory Piatetsky-Shapiro, Ph.D., is a well-known expert in business analytics, data mining, and data science. He is the editor and publisher of KDnuggets.com, a co-founder of KDD (Knowledge Discovery and Data mining conferences), and SIGKDD (a professional organization for Knowledge Discovery and Data Mining).

11 http://www.kdnuggets.com/2014/01/split-on-data-science-skills-individual-vs-team-approach.html

Business expertise:

- An **information technology specialist** who will oversee implementation of the model in a production environment
- One or more **subject-matter experts (SMEs)** who will serve as interfaces between the technical workers building the model and the business users of the model. SMEs provide critically important information about the organization's technology and goals, the meaning of data, and the reasonableness of a model's output. Without input from SMEs, data scientists can sometimes get lost in the theoretical and lose touch with the practical.
- One or more **champions** who will provide leadership for the cultural transformation and training aspects of the project
- A **project manager** (for larger projects) who will schedule the various project activities and serve as an interface between the various members of the team

When clients engage our services for a medium- to large-scale project, we will typically furnish a project manager and team members for the "data expertise" category above, and the client will provide the majority of the "business expertise" members. Clients with considerable experience in data analytics may also contribute some of their own personnel to the "data expertise" category.

Because the needs of a project will vary as it progresses, only part of the crew assigned to the project will actually be working on it at any one time. This "personnel as needed" approach gives our clients a high level of service at lower costs.

Often there is overlap among these various functions. For example, some software engineers may cross over from development into modeling, and some modelers might do some development work. On smaller projects, the lead data scientist may also serve as the project manager.

Assembling the Team

When building a data analytics team, it's important to consider temperaments as well as skills and knowledge. For example, every team needs a visionary who can generate enthusiasm, a high-level architect who can plan the work, and some workhorses who are good with detail. It's been our experience that teams whose members have diverse temperaments produce better dynamics.

Other members of the team should include a person responsible for getting data to the analytics people, at least one SME who can answer questions about the organization as they arise, and the person who will be responsible for implementing the changes that will result from the analytics work. Ideally, the person in charge of deploying the model should be an active member of the team from the beginning. The continual guidance provided by this person about the practicality of proposed changes and the advantages or disadvantages of proposed ideas will facilitate buy-in and promote ultimate success.

From the very beginning of the analytics initiative, it is crucial to identify the likely sources of the data that will be needed and to bring on board the people who will be responsible for making that data available. Some of these people may be custodians of needed data, who can understand the data as well as supply it. Other team members might simply serve as liaisons or coordinators for purposes of obtaining data from multiple sources and supplying it to the analytics project.

The people responsible for supplying data, who might be from IT, HR, sales, finance, or other areas of the organization, need not be on-going active members of the team. After furnishing the requested data, some may have little or no continuing involvement with the project. Other data custodians may have important on-going roles. After furnishing the initial data, they may occasionally stay involved to provide new datasets and to answer questions about the data they've provided, so modelers can understand it. Data providers are essential, especially in the early stages of the project.

BRYAN'S STORY
Part 2: Staffing a Data Analytics Project

Starting out, we had a very small team, and many on the team really weren't excited about their involvement. Fortunately, there was some enthusiasm around solving problems related to worker's compensation, health care, and claimant program issues. These were a big concern to management, and they'd been trying to manage them for a number of years.

We were fortunate that the head of our agency, Dave Williams, was a visionary, and he had seen and read enough about analytics to know that it would be useful for law enforcement. He set the course, got buy-in from some of the other senior leaders in the organization, and made sure we had the initial resources we needed. He also assigned an investigator to be the subject-matter expert member of our team, which was crucial. Then he got out of the way and let those of us who were responsible for the work do what we needed to do. In many respects, he was an ideal leader.

I quickly realized that government did not have people with the necessary skill sets in data science. We were fortunate to come into contact with Elder Research, and we used a modest portion of our budget to get them and another consultant, IHS Global Insight, started with us. Bringing in data analytics consultants to supplement our work was critical to our success.

I found people who had intriguing business problems and were willing to take a bit of a risk by working with us. I'd say, "Here's what we want to do, and if we do it this way, you should expect a return on investment of this."

What is a Data Scientist?

"We can make a data scientist out of anybody in five minutes," boasted the CEO of a data analytics software company in a presentation we recently attended. That was an unbelievable claim! While the software tool this vendor markets is indeed useful for performing an initial analysis of data, and it can indeed make an analyst more productive, it absolutely cannot turn a data analyst into a data scientist.

Actually, even the term "data scientist" is confusing. "It's time to kill the title 'data scientist,'" suggests Thomas Davenport, Distinguished Professor in Information Technology and Management at Babson College and

Director of Research at the International Institute for Analytics.[12] "The data scientist term, which originally stood for quantitative experts who could also do a lot of the computational wizardry involved in analyzing unstructured Big Data, has come to mean almost anything," Davenport goes on to say. "In addition to basic quantitative analysts, I've seen it applied to database administrator jobs, programmer jobs, and web development jobs. I've seen it applied to jobs requiring a PhD, an MBA or Masters in analytics, or a BA 'in some quantitative field.'"

A lot of people who can perform many of the functions within the first four levels of analytics described in the second chapter of this book label themselves data scientists, but levels five through ten, the true domain of data scientists, are beyond their capabilities. In our view, data scientists must understand and be able to work with highly sophisticated quantitative techniques, such as probabilistic graphical methods, neural networks, logistic regression, decision trees, analysis of variance (ANOVA), polynomial networks, nearest neighbors, and complex network analysis. They will have undergraduate degrees in engineering, computer science, math, statistics, or some other quantitative field of study, and most will hold advanced degrees. A rough popular definition is that data scientists know more about statistics than a computer scientist and more about software development than a statistician.

In the early days of data mining, when few universities offered data analytics curriculums, we typically had to devote more than a year to bringing a new hire up to an acceptable level of productivity. In the past few years, however, many programs for training data scientists have sprung up around the country. Northwestern University, Georgetown University, Columbia University, and Louisiana State University all have excellent curriculums, and the University of Virginia is building an extensive program. Several members of our firm are graduates of the Institute of Advanced Analytics at North Carolina State University, which is currently the leading training institution in the field.

Nevertheless, even when graduates from these and other top institutions come to us with excellent academic training in data analytics, we find that we still must do quite a bit of additional training about our own processes. We especially must teach our new team members how to test and verify models so we will all have confidence in the accuracy levels we report

---

12 The *CIO Journal,* an online publication of the *Wall Street Journal,* April 30, 2014

to clients. We suspect you will encounter the same situation if and when you decide to build your own data analytics capability.

More than Academic Credentials

While academic studies provide an important foundation for the practice of data science, they alone do not make a good data scientist. Academic knowledge must be augmented with experience. For example, we are not aware of any academic program that adequately teaches project validation. This is a key aspect of successful data science, as we will explain in Chapter 11.

A good data scientist must have an understanding of statistics, mathematics, and programming, but even the best education doesn't guarantee success. Over the years, we've seen some very smart people with excellent technical skills struggle with the practical application of the concepts. We first noticed this phenomenon several years ago, when we hired three summer interns to work with one of our most experienced data scientists.

One of these interns was a semester away from completing his master's degree in statistics at a top university; the second had just earned his bachelor's degree in chemical engineering from one of the leading universities in the country; and the third was an economics major who had just finished his sophomore year of college. Over the course of the summer, the undergraduate economics major was the only one who demonstrated a high level of competence. This surprised us because this fellow had the least amount of formal education. We don't normally think of economics as the ideal preparation for data science, but he seemed to have the type of brain that "got" what we did. Even though all three interns were equally bright, two of them simply didn't "click" with the profession.

The best data scientists tend to be naturally inquisitive. They're not afraid to ask questions that may appear foolish in order to learn about a company's operations. They have the ability to communicate effectively with senior-level management and translate the everyday language of business into the quantitative language of analytical modeling.

By now, it should be obvious why good data scientists are in short supply. Data science is a highly complex field that requires considerable knowledge and experience, along with a certain "knack." You can't just go out and hire college graduates who majored in statistics and expect them to do a credible job.

The Most Important Quality

The key quality we always look for when hiring data scientists is humility. The best team members are willing to suspend their own opinions and preferences and listen to the views of others. They are better learners because they don't think they know everything and they're not afraid to ask questions that might make them look foolish. They usually make better teachers because they don't come across as arrogant. And because they are unashamedly inquisitive, colleagues are more willing to ask them questions and engage them in dialog.

Data analytics is largely a trial-and-error process. Every problem is different. There are no formulae that always work, and no one solution is best for every problem. The most successful data scientists are willing to try different approaches and risk short-term failure. They have the humility to question their own work and accept input from others. To them, acceptable is not good enough. They keep refining their models, driven by their natural curiosity, until they achieve the best solution possible within given time and budget constraints.

Diversity of experience is a big asset when working on a data analytics project. We have people at our firm who have worked with financial institutions, government agencies, pharmaceutical companies, insurance companies, petrochemical companies, and many other types of organizations in such diverse areas as fraud detection, credit scoring, cross selling, risk scoring and process optimization. Whiteboards cover the walls of our offices, and we encourage our data scientists and software engineers to use them for brainstorming with their counterparts from other teams. This cross-collaboration among professionals working in different industries pays big dividends.

Many people have difficulty asking for and accepting input from others, especially from those who are relatively young, inexperienced, or junior in organizational rank. In some companies, it's a sign of weakness to ask for help, but "Lone Ranger" data scientists who try to look like they have all the answers seldom produce outstanding results. They will sometimes struggle for months on a problem before they realize they're on the wrong track. If they had been willing to collaborate, they could have saved considerable time and money.

Although we have job titles at Elder Research, we strive to keep authority levels from interfering with the exchange of information. We want our very junior people to feel free to respectfully challenge the thinking of even the senior members of the organization. Mike Thurber's story illustrates how this works.

MIKE THURBER'S STORY

On Fridays, Elder Research has a "tech talk," when someone presents an idea or a case study to the data scientists and software engineers in the company. I still vividly remember the first one I attended. Although I was new to the company, I had worked for many years in the field of data analytics for a very large financial institution based in New York City. The presenter on this particular day was a senior member of Elder Research. At that time he was in his early fifties, and he had close to thirty years of industry experience.

Soon after this senior data scientist began his talk, some people started peppering him with challenging questions. Their tone was respectful, but their questions and comments were direct. They would say things like, "Have you thought about this?" or "I think you might have overlooked something there."

I was shocked. The people asking the questioners were young. A few were just out of college, and some might even have been college interns. At my former company, the culture had been rigid and hierarchical. People were very conscious of position and no one would have ever dared to question the ideas and decisions of senior leaders.

I noticed, however, that none in attendance considered these questions impertinent. I was very impressed with the presenter's humility. He would say things like, "Thank you. I didn't think of that. I'll give that a try." I later learned that Elder Research encourages team members to respectfully challenge each other. It is an important aspect of the company's culture. I was very excited to have landed at a place that so highly values the utility of ideas, regardless of the source.

Building Teams through "Gap Analysis"

In addition to making our data analytics teams available to solve our clients' problems, we sometimes help our clients build their own internal data analytics teams. For example, a federal agency that was just getting started in data analytics recently asked us to work with their six-person analytics team to identify any gaps that might exist in the skill sets of their people, the suitability of their data, and the capabilities of their analytics tools. This client wanted to assign these six people to four teams, so each person would be serving on two teams. They asked us to help them make the assignments.

As we looked at the backgrounds of these six people, we found that they had a good mix of business experience. A couple of them had some skill at data science, one at the master's level. At our suggestion, the agency had come up with a list of fifteen possible projects, and we settled on four that required the application of a wide range of analytics methods.

When making the team assignments, we took the backgrounds of the six team members into account. For instance, we noticed that one team member had geospatial experience, so we assigned him to a project with a geospatial component. We also made sure that no two people served together on more than one team. This encouraged some healthy team dynamics, and it ensured that each project benefited from a breadth of experience.

This is essentially the way we staff our own company projects. We also try to take strengths and weaknesses into account as we assign people to teams, so that one person's weaknesses are complemented by another person's strengths.

As part of the "gap analysis" for this client, we are building four models that will enable them to move their future analytics initiatives from the identification of the business problem to the operationalization of the analytics solution. While installing these models, we will train the agency's team on a number of different techniques. This is a novel approach to building an analytics team, and we suspect that we will be doing more of this kind of knowledge transfer in the future.

A good team consists of more than a few data analytics experts and a champion. It includes people who understand the business and the data, and people who are going to be using the model. Involving a wide range of people from the beginning increases buy-in, which increases the probability of using the results, and therefore the probability of success.

Chapter Nuggets

- Data science is a highly complex discipline that requires a diversity of skills.
- When building a data analytics team, it's important to consider temperaments as well as skills and knowledge.
- Every team needs a visionary who can generate enthusiasm, a high-level architect who can plan the work, and some workhorses who are good with detail.
- Data scientists must understand and be able to work with highly sophisticated quantitative techniques, such as graphical methods, neural networks, logistic regression, decision trees, and nearest neighbors. They will typically have undergraduate degrees in engineering, computer science, math, statistics, or some other quantitative field of study, and many will hold advanced degrees.
- The best data scientists are naturally inquisitive. They're not afraid to ask questions that may appear foolish in order to learn about a company's operations, and they are willing to try different approaches, even at the risk of short-term failure. They have the ability to communicate effectively with senior-level management and translate the everyday language of business into the quantitative language of analytical modeling.

CHAPTER 5

ACQUIRING THE RIGHT TOOLS

Software tools are an essential component of data analytics. It's exciting to shop for the right ones, but beware! Don't let the enchanting bells and whistles of the alluring software packages and the persuasive pitches of software salespeople fool you into thinking that fancy tools will make your organizations analytically competent. That will never happen.

The information in this chapter will help you better understand the types of tools available, so you can make better purchasing decisions. Before you rush out and buy software, however, assess your needs and assemble your analytics team. We recommend hiring a data analytics consultant to help you define the problems you need to solve and the type of software you need to solve them. This kind of assessment and planning can save you a lot of money when purchasing the software. And because the software will better match your needs, you'll enjoy a much higher return on your investment over the long run. A few years ago a large pharmaceutical company hired us to provide training on an expensive analytics tool they had purchased six months earlier. When we arrived, management couldn't find the software. After a company-wide search, someone finally found the package on a shelf. The hastily purchased software had become *shelfware*. Unfortunately, this is a common occurrence in many organizations.

The snazzy features of many analytics software packages can make it easy to overbuy. Some people, new to the field of analytics, imitate the car buyer who goes into the dealership intending to purchase a basic vehicle for driving around town, but ends up driving away in a luxury car with a big engine, leather seats, satellite radio, and lots of non-essential features.

When purchasing physical assets, such as office space or plant machinery, it's appropriate to think long term. Analytics tools are different. The field is constantly evolving, so it's impractical to try to plan five years ahead. It's better to start small and stay nimble, so you can take advantage of new developments as they become available. If you've invested millions of dollars in a particular tool and a hundred thousand dollars more in training people on it, you may be reluctant to discontinue using it, even when your requirements change or more advanced tools come along. We recommend buying for your currents needs, and then adding software as your needs change. Stay flexible, and don't lock yourself in to a particular tool or vendor.

The strategy of starting small and adding software as you go also encourages your analytics personnel to keep abreast of advancements in the field. In addition to producing better analytics results, this approach usually translates into greater professional growth, skills proficiency, and job satisfaction for your team.

Some companies, new to data analytics, overemphasize the importance of having the right tools, and they underestimate the importance of having the people with the right knowledge and experience to use them effectively. There are many excellent data analytics tools on the market, but even the best ones have limited value if the people using them lack experience in the science and practice of analytics.

A Variety of Techniques and Disciplines

Figure 5-1, developed by our colleagues John Elder and Dustin Hux, depicts the constantly shifting landscape of analytics techniques organized by discipline. Notice that some techniques, such as polynomial networks, are used in only one discipline (in this case, data mining), while others, such as neural networks or time series analysis, are applied in multiple disciplines.

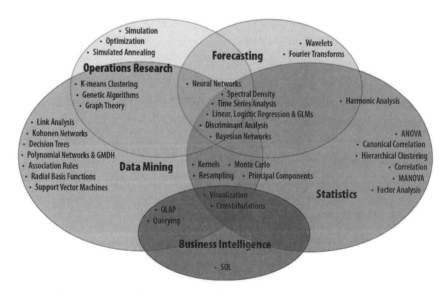

Figure 5-1: Leading Analytic Techniques and their Disciplines

Every tool has strengths and weaknesses. Some, such as those provided by SAS and by IBM/SPSS, cover a broad range of these techniques, but no one tool meets all needs. So, when purchasing software, first determine which techniques will best match your problem. Then choose the tool or tools that best perform these techniques. This will maximize return on investment and reduce the likelihood of ending up with "shelfware." The nature of the problems should drive your procurement decision, not the appeal of the software.

Analytics tools can also be classified according to the types of processes they perform. The basic four types, as shown in Figure 5-2, are (1) extract, transfer, and load (ETL); (2) standardization; (3) analytics; and (4) visualization.

- **ETL analytics tools** *extract, transform,* and *load* project data from different sources in order to reduce redundancy and build data audit capabilities. For example, if one data source contains the physical description of a person, and another dataset contains information about the person's educational background, a standard ETL tool can link these two tables using a common data key field, such as social security number. Popular ETL tools include Clover, Scriptella, KETL, Pentaho, Oracle Data Integrator, and IBM Datastage. Many people also use programming languages such as SQL and Java to perform ETL.

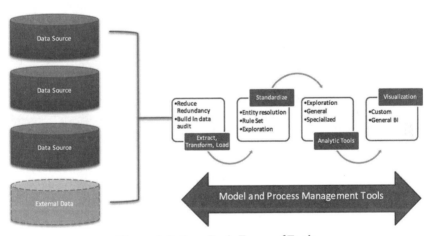

Figure 5-2: Four Basic Types of Tools

If the two sets of data do not contain a common key field, the data scientist may need to employ a more powerful ETL technique that uses an analytical methodology called "entity resolution." This technique might be needed, for example, to link an educational background record, which contains an individual's Social Security number, with the person's Facebook page, which does not.

- **Data standardization tools** are specialized kinds of ETL tools that clean and standardize incoming data. For example, the word "street" is sometimes abbreviated in address fields as "St.," and the word "avenue" is sometimes abbreviated "Ave." A data standardization tool can convert these different spellings into a uniform format according to rules dictated by the data scientist. SAS DataFlux is a popular data standardization tool.

- **Data exploration tools** help the analyst quickly explore the data. These tools are most helpful when the analyst already has a set of questions to ask the data. They are less helpful for discovering the questions to ask, and they are not the best tools for separating needles (interesting data) from the haystack (total data sample). Scriptella, KETL, Pentaho, Oracle Data Integrator, and IBM Datastage are some good examples.

- **General analytics tools** manipulate data and apply a set of common statistical and data mining techniques to it. These techniques include link analysis, decision trees, and principal components. Examples include SAS, IBM/SPSS, Statistica, and R.

- **Specialized analytics tools** are most often used with such disciplines as operations research and forecasting. Examples include Gurobi, a linear programming tool for optimization, and Netica, a tool that supports graphical creation and evaluation of Bayesian networks.

- **Visualization tools** display data and analytics in an intuitive way that allows the consumer of the information to more easily understand and act on it. There are

> **Business Intelligence (BI) tools** span several areas, including data exploration, general analytics, and visualization. They are designed to help create reports and visual dashboards easily through an intuitive point and click interface.

so many of these tools available that it's difficult to name just a few, though popular ones include JMP (a SAS product) and Tableau. Many of the tools we've already mentioned have a visualization component, which may be included or available as an optional feature.

- **Model management tools** provide an orderly and efficient mechanism for updating models to conform to technological advances, changes in the business environment, and changes in application specifications. Models are usually composed of multiple components (ETL tools, data standardization tools, visualization tools, etc.), all of which are interrelated. Changes to one module will affect the others. Model management tools provide version control and configuration management capabilities, so analytics models can be kept up to date. These tools may be specifically configured or purchased as standard packages. SAS and IBM/SPSS both provide model management tools, but there is also an open-source option, Kuri, developed by Elder Research.

- **Big data tools** allow models to access and analyze large volumes of data, especially data created at high velocity, which require more than one computer to store or process it. An example of such an application might be the real-time monitoring of nationwide credit card transactions. Generally, big data tools employ distributed data and processing to divide one data set into chunks to make progress in parallel on multiple computers. After processing, they reconstitute the individual pieces into an overall analytic solution. Teradata and Greenplum are two of the better-known suppliers of big data hardware and software. Hadoop is a popular open-source software package, which can be implemented on low-cost commodity hardware to help manage the processing of distributed data. Leading examples of open-source software packages (all under the Apache umbrella) include Spark, Hive, and Hadoop. The latter might be considered the kernel for a larger set of open-source software.

Interface Level of Tools

Analytics tools also can be classified according to the following two interface levels:

1. **Command line interfaces** give the user more control and flexibility for manipulating files. They are lower-level tools that may require considerable knowledge and training to use. To borrow an analogy from the personal computer world, command line interfaces might be compared to Microsoft DOS, while wrappers might be compared to the Windows operating system.

   Below are examples of command line interfaces and open-source libraries, in no particular order:
   - **R** – An object-oriented, open-source set of programming tool packages
   - **Python** – An open-source scripting language gaining popularity in data mining
   - **Scala** – A general-purpose, open-source programming language that incorporates programming concepts that are both object-oriented and functional.
   - **Apache** – A suite of open-source tools built around big data concepts. Hadoop is one of the core libraries in the suite. Spark, a large-scale data processing engine, is another library that is growing rapidly in popularity.

- Base SAS – The base statistical software package offered by SAS. (SAS is the largest independent vendor in the business intelligence market.[13])
- IBM/SPSS Statistics Standard – The base statistical package offered by IBM/ SPSS (an integrated family of products that addresses the entire analytical process.[14])

2. **Wrappers** are higher-level tools with sophisticated graphical user interfaces (GUI) that free data scientists to focus their attention on the analytics problems instead of on the software programming details. In the context of software development, wrappers might be called integrated development environments (IDEs). They make it possible for data scientists to program "analytic streams" by dragging and dropping components and then linking model components into a work stream using a visual interface, much like the popular program WordPress makes it possible for people to design websites without using HTML.

Below are some popular wrappers, listed in no particular order:

- **Statistica Data Miner** – Created by Statsoft, Inc. (now owned by a private equity firm)
- **IBM/SPSS Modeler** – An IBM product built on the SPSS Statistics platform
- **SAS Enterprise Miner** – A SAS product built on the SAS Base software with additional algorithms and functionality
- **Rapid Miner** – A RapidMiner, Inc. data mining product built on R
- **Knime** (pronounced "nime") – An increasingly popular open-source tool built using Java with fees for increased functionality

When evaluating tools, don't be unduly swayed by the sophistication of their graphics. We've seen some companies purchase analytics software primarily because they were impressed with the way they displayed results. A powerful GUI is nice to have, but first make sure the software does the job.

---

13 http://www.SAS.com

14 http://www-01.ibm.com/software/analytics/spss/products/statistics/

BRYAN'S STORY
Part 3: Acquiring the Right Tools

I think one of the mistakes that many businesses make is focusing too much on purchasing a tool, instead of trying to understand the right tool. They go out and spend way too much money on tools they don't really understand. It was difficult to hold the line on this because the leadership in our organization kept bringing in vendors and suggesting that we buy these things that other organizations had bought. I had to push back on spending money too soon. Later on, when we knew more about data analytics and our own needs, we would go out and look for certain tools, instead of waiting for vendors to bombard us with sales pitches about tools we didn't need.

On this project we felt the best approach was to develop our own visualization tools. With the help of Elder Research, we cycled through the development of several very quickly. About once a week we'd come up with a new prototype, and investigators could choose the one that best matched their personal preference and the problem they were trying to solve. These customized tools were so much better than the one-size-fits-all products that a lot of analytics vendors try to sell. It's been my experience that government agencies typically pay a lot of money for standardized tools, and then they utilize only about one percent of their capability. Sometimes users will try to force these standardized tools to fit problems they weren't designed to solve.

Sources of Tools

Analytics tools can also be classified according to their source:

- **Open-source tools** are generally created by "hobbyists." Many of these hobbyists are professional software developers who survey the commercial tools on the market and decide there must be a better way. When one open-source creator puts an interesting idea out in the public domain, other developers hop on board and contribute their ideas. All donate their time for the thrill of the creative process and the satisfaction of producing something useful.

  There are a number of very good open-source programs on the market, and more are introduced all the time. The high-level programming languages R and Python are especially sophisticated and widely used. They can be a good option for small organizations or for organizations that are just getting started in data analytics. Interestingly, we are starting to see some larger businesses and some organizations with more established analytics services look toward the enterprise versions of these open-source tools. Revolution R is an example of an enterprise-ready implementation of R offered commercially. We are beginning to see many more creators of open-source tools offer their enterprise-ready versions for sale.

- Commercial analytics tools are larger and more sophisticated software programs offered by commercial software vendors. Bigger organizations with substantial data analytics needs typically purchase one or more these types of tools. They come with a wide range of capabilities and prices. An organization that needs tools for each of its various business units might spend several million dollars in leasing fees per year.

  SAS is perhaps the largest and best-known supplier of commercial analytics tools. They offer a very broad tool set for a wide range of applications. IBM, the other huge supplier of commercial analytics tools, sells a popular tool in the wrapper category called Modeler. Statistica, another well know wrapper, was recently sold by Dell to a private equity firm. Many other smaller, niche suppliers should not be ignored. For instance, KXEN is a tool that is designed to build and manage hundreds of robust models automatically, where each model is for a separate, well-defined subset of the data. This fits the needs of credit card agencies very well, for example, where each data subset might be a distinct category of purchases, such as travel expenses.

A Word about Open-Source Tools

Open-source tools represent a popular and growing segment of the analytic domain, because they cost little or nothing to acquire, and they are usually on the cutting edge technologically. We recommend that all analytic teams include them in their toolset, but keep in mind that it does cost something to learn how to use them and to maintain the work created in them.

It's unfortunate that quite a few IT departments resist using open-source software. Usually they cite security concerns and lack of service-level support agreements as reasons. Also, most organizations require that software must first be tested and approved before it can be deployed on their networks. Commercial vendors provide the necessary information and resources to gain this approval, but with open-source tools the IT department or the sponsoring internal organization must shoulder the entire burden. The Knime tool has a fee-based version that is supported, and we see this as a middle road that other tools will follow.

Admittedly, gaining IT approval can require quite a bit of work. For example, when helping a federal government client proceed through this process, our firm had to complete multiple documents exceeding fifty pages each! Nevertheless, we believe that the value of open-source software makes this effort worthwhile. Beware of IT departments that play the security-vulnerability card as a scare tactic to avoid the work involved in testing and approving open-source software.

Commercial vendors also generally have a bias against open-source tools, but for a different reason: they are afraid these free products will siphon off market share from their commercial products. We believe, though, that the extent of this threat is limited. In fact, commercial vendors can leverage these open-source tools by incorporating the more promising techniques into their own products.

Recently, open-source developers have become more adept at protecting their creations. In most cases, even when the basic free software is protected, commercial firms can add wrappers and other features to turn these tools into viable commercial products. In fact, an argument can be made that open-source software benefits commercial vendors because it allows them to develop new products more rapidly, while saving them millions of dollars in R&D.

Tool Trends

We anticipate that software tools will continue to become increasingly sophisticated, and that companies will design more and more of them for niche markets. In the future we expect to see suppliers focus most of their development efforts on the following types of tools:

- **Sophisticated tools** to facilitate the use of multiple single tables and the construction of relational multi-table analytic data sets
- **Visualization tools** to make data easier to understand and use
- **Wrapper tools** to further automate the data analytics process, so the data scientist can spend more time understanding the problem and less time dealing with programming details

Many good exploratory analytics tools are available for working with tabular data. Far fewer descriptive and predictive analytics tools are available for working with sequential and relational data.

- **Tabular data** is the most common form of data used for analytics. It is primarily stored for record-keeping purposes. For example, a tabular format might be used to store a list of customers and information about those customers.

- **Sequential data** is transactional in nature. For example, it might include a list of orders submitted over a period of time with timestamps showing when they were received and shipped, a list of daily stock prices by date, or a set of repeated measurements that occur over time, such as blood pressure readings for an individual.

- **Relational data** is in a form that enables the exploration of relationships in the data and the visualization of those relationships. From this data it is easy to find out which entities share a common identifier, such as a phone number. The connection data of "friends" on Facebook is perhaps the most common form of relational data.

- **Text data** is believed to be the most abundant form of data in the world[15]. People sometime mistakenly think of text mining as a model-building method. A better way to think about text mining is as a super-data-prep exercise. The goal of text mining is to transform unstructured text data into a structured format that can be used to generate new features for models.

Causal analytics tools represent a frontier that is ripe for development. Attributing cause is very challenging. It is quite common for inexperienced data scientists to conclude mistakenly that B is causing A, when in fact B may simply be correlated with A. More rigorous analytics might show, for example, that although A is correlated with B, it is actually caused by C, D, E, and F.

In this chapter we have just scratched the surface on the types of tools that are available, but this overview should provide you with a basic understanding for making wise purchasing decisions. Providing more detail would be counterproductive because the field is changing so rapidly.

When it comes time to purchase software, we recommend hiring an analytics consultant who has experience with several types of software. A consultant will help you look "under the hood" of the multiple analytics tools you are considering and identify those best suited to solve your business problems. How a tool works is far more important than how it looks. Resist the urge to overbuy. Make sure you have people on your team who possess the technical understanding to use the software you purchase.

---

15 For a more detailed discussion on different types of data, see Section 4.0 Advanced Data Types in *The Ten Levels of Analytics* booklet by Andrew Fast, Ph.D. and John Elder, Ph.D, which is also referenced in Chapter 2. This is available by download at http://www.MiningYourOwnBusiness.com.

Chapter Nuggets

- The enchanting bells and whistles of software packages and the persuasive pitches of software suppliers' salespeople can lure the analytically inexperienced into thinking that fancy tools will make an organization analytically competent. That's never the case!

- Some companies new to data analytics overemphasize the importance of having the right tools, and they underestimate the importance of having the people with the right knowledge and experience to use them effectively.

- Open-source tools are a popular and growing segment of the analytic domain. They cost little or nothing to obtain, and they are usually on the cutting edge technologically.

- We anticipate that software tools will continue to increase in sophistication, and that companies will design more and more of them for niche markets.

CHAPTER 6

HIRING DATA ANALYTICS CONSULTANTS

In the earliest days of data analytics, our new clients would typically say, "Solve this problem for us." As they saw the enduring power of analytics, their request then became, "We want to launch our own data analytics capability. Will you help us set it up?"

However, growing an analytics capability from scratch is a huge challenge, and today more companies appreciate its difficulty. Instead of expecting an analytics consultant to come in, tell them what to do, and then leave, knowledgeable organizations say, "Come in, and help us solve this problem. If you do a good job, we'll ask you to help us with other problems. Meanwhile, we'd like your support over the long run as we set up our own analytics capability."

Launching into data analytics without professional assistance usually leads to trouble. Most organizations need quite a bit of help over a substantial period of time before they can "take off the training wheels." Even companies with considerable experience in the field usually require ongoing professional support with the hard science around recent advances. You can waste a great deal of time and money trying to go it alone. And the costs really soar if a weak model leads to erroneous decisions!

If your organization intends to rely on data science on a consistent and growing basis, you will likely want to build your own in-house analytics capability. Do it gradually. Don't rush out and start hiring data scientists. Engage a consultant to help you define your needs and develop a plan to meet them. The knowledge you gain by working with a consultant will benefit you over the long run, and in the short run you'll do a better job of planning and staffing your analytics initiative. Also, early successes will serve to protect the initiative against competing budget priorities.

A large government agency recently asked us to help them decide whether they should increase their analytics capability by hiring more people or by expanding their use of consultants. After identifying the problems they wanted to solve and assessing their staff, tools, and data, we made a recommendation that allowed them to meet their needs in the most cost-effective manner. If they had launched into their expansion without this assessment, they could have wasted money on buying the wrong kind of software or hiring the wrong kind of people.

Discerning Fact from Hype

There are many types of consultants in the analytics world, and unfortunately some may not be what they seem. A few intentionally try to inflate their capabilities, but the main problem stems from the complexity and fluidity of the field of data science, where the definitions of key roles can be confusing, and the demarcation lines between disciplines are blurred. Some consultants honestly believe they are doing one thing, when actually they are doing something different.

When you're hiring consultants, you may have to wade through hype. Many consulting companies that offer business intelligence (BI) services accept higher-level analytics engagements in hopes that they can figure out what's needed as they go along.

At a recent high-level analytics conference we attended, the organizing committee had invited a man to speak who was supposed to be an expert on predictive analytics and data mining. He had an excellent title for his presentation, and his credentials seemed impressive. Soon after he began to speak, however, it was obvious he was talking about basic descriptive analysis, not predictive analytics. Better vetting would have revealed that this man's analytics work was not up to the level expected at this conference, but apparently no one on the committee had taken the time to ask him hard questions.

If experts who run analytics conferences have trouble identifying the right speaker, you may be wondering how you will ever be able to hire the right consultant. Actually, the chances of doing a good job of hiring are solid, if you do your homework. Your first homework assignment is to learn enough about data analytics to be able to separate fact from hype. Reading this book gives you a good start with that, and we've listed some additional resources for further study on the book's website, *www.MiningYourOwnBusiness.com*.

The second homework assignment is to do a thorough job of interviewing prospective consultants. Ask them what types of problems they have solved, and verify the results by checking references. Find out how they manage projects and evaluate their answers in light of what you learned in Chapters 3 and 4. Ask them what tools they use (see Chapter 5). Inquire about their data mining process, comparing their answer to what you will read in Chapter 7.

Recently we had conversations with the CEOs of two firms whose websites promoted their analytics services. We knew that they specialized only in IT services, so we politely inquired about what types of analytics they performed. Both told us that they didn't do analytics, but they felt they had to put the term "analytics" on their website to get respect.

We didn't pursue the matter further, but we wondered how they would respond to clients who actually asked for analytics services. Perhaps they would subcontract the work to a firm that specializes in analytics, but more likely they would do some elaborate spreadsheet and metrics-based work and call it advanced analytics. Most customers new to analytics wouldn't be able to distinguish the difference while the work was in progress, unless perhaps they'd read this book!

BRYAN'S STORY
Part 4: Hiring Analytics Consultants

Companies were constantly trying to get us to buy their analytics consulting services. There was a lot of hype and very little substance, and most of what they were selling didn't fit our needs. A lot of these consultants were big companies that provided twenty different types of services other than analytics, and they had added analytics as another business line simply because it is an up-and-coming thing. When it really came down to it, their salesmen couldn't even explain what analytics was.

The consultants we hired, on the other hand, came in and talked with us about what problem we wanted to solve, what data and other resources we had, and other key issues. They didn't try to sell us a tool, a software package, or even their consulting services. They assessed the landscape and then formulated a plan about how we could best solve our problem.

Evaluating Industry Experience

In most cases, it's not necessary or even particularly helpful for the consultant to have experience in your specific industry. In most cases, "data is data." An analytics technique that works in one domain (industry) will work fine with the same type of application in another domain. However, the consultants must be willing to listen to you and employ your domain expertise to best effect. Beware if they assume their magic software will take the place of domain knowledge.

A few years ago, a huge credit card company, well known for its analytics proficiency, inquired about our services. They had over one hundred masters-level and PhD-level statisticians working full time to build models to score credit risk, but a leader had forced them to reach outside to see if any of these new-fangled data mining techniques had anything of value to add to their expertise. The team who contacted us was cool and reserved, because involving us would be a blow to their pride. Also, they were skeptical about our ability to help, because we didn't specialize in the credit card industry.

The president of our firm, John Elder, sensing their low expectations and reluctance, offered them a wager. He said, "We will build ten models testing ten different mining technologies at half the agreed-upon charge. If any does worse than the models your experts build, you owe us nothing more, and you will have learned a path not likely to produce gain. If any does better, however, you pay us double our fee for that model."

The company readily accepted the challenge, because they were the modeling experts within the credit card industry, and they welcomed the chance to recoup half the budget they were being forced to spend. Fortunately, the cooperation we received from the client's scientists in explaining the key data fields and their interrelationships and limits ensured that our modeling efforts had a sporting chance.

It turned out that in seven of the ten cases, our models were demonstrably better than the ones they had been using, and our ensembles of the models were better still. Even though most of our team had no experience in the credit card industry, we were able to surpass the performance of their experts who worked in that industry day after day. Our lack of industry experience actually helped, because it allowed us to see the problem with fresh eyes. Our data modeling experience with many other types of businesses also enabled us to think of creative solutions that had not occurred to these industry-specific experts. In the end, company management was extremely happy because the increased accuracy of our models almost immediately produced tens of millions of dollars in gains for their operations.

Certain firms specialize in providing data analytics services in narrowly defined areas, such as credit card scoring, insurance risk scoring, or web analytics. Because of specialization, they are sometimes able to develop automated systems and other techniques to increase their cost-effectiveness. If you have such an "analytically mature" application area, you might want to check out vendors that specialize in your industry. Still, don't assume that such a firm is automatically the best choice. A strong data analytics consultant, unfamiliar with your specific problem area, can often take a fresh look at your need and come up with a new and better solution.

Evaluating Analytics Experience

Although experience in your organization's industry generally isn't necessary, experience in analytics definitely is. Evaluating a consultant's sophistication in analytics can be tricky, however. When hiring consultants, it's especially important to understand the difference between data analytics and business intelligence.

Data analytics relates to Levels 5 through 10 on the hierarchy of analytics outlined in Chapter 2. It involves the use of very sophisticated analytical techniques, such as clustering, predictive modeling, text mining, or link analysis.

Business intelligence (BI), on the other hand, relates more to traditional descriptive analysis and advanced spreadsheets. It is useful for transforming raw data into meaningful information for business analysis and decision-making, but it is far less powerful than data analytics. Make sure the consultant you hire matches the need you have.

By the way, software sales people generally don't make good analytics consultants. They have enough knowledge and experience to sell their own software, but very few are qualified to help clients define analytics problems and develop and deploy holistic solutions.

Recently, an organization asked us to help them with a particular challenge. We assigned two of our experienced people to the problem, and they solved it in less than two months. The client then informed us that a team of data scientists from another consulting firm had been working on a simplified version of this problem for almost a year without success. This other vendor was one of the most highly respected consulting firms in the world in their specialty. The problem was simply that their specialty was BI, not data analytics.

Finding the Right Consultant

Where do you search for a reliable vendor of analytics services? One good way is to attend analytics conferences. You can learn a lot at these conferences by listening to the speakers, visiting the exhibits, and talking with other participants. For example, Predictive Analytics World (PAW) annually sponsors approximately a dozen high-level conferences in major cities around North America and in Europe. PAW, which is arguably the best entry-level conference, encourages the presentation of case studies that address business as well as technical issues. Your most technical people may enjoy the depth of more academic conferences, such as KDD (Knowledge Discovery and Data Mining) or ICDM (IEEE Conference on Data Mining).

Another idea is to talk with companies that have successfully used analytics. Unless they directly compete with you, they should be willing to give you some helpful advice.

We said in this chapter and in other parts of this book that the data scientists working on your problem don't need to be an expert in your field, and they probably don't even need to have basic knowledge about your field. That doesn't mean expertise is unnecessary. A complete project team will include at least one subject-matter expert (SME) who does have deep knowledge of the domain. Depending on the complexity of the project, other SMEs might be needed for the various technical issues being addressed and the processes involved.

The work that our company did for a large petrochemical company included multiple SMEs. One had detailed knowledge of the process for drilling natural gas wells, and another was an expert in operating the wells after the digging was completed. Another SME, who knew how the natural gas moved from the wells to the market, was also engaged. The client company provided all of these SMEs at minimal cost. None was needed anywhere close to full time over the course of the project; most simply contributed an hour or two a week to answer questions as they arose from the data scientists. Weeks went by without any involvement from some SMEs.

Most projects require subject-matter expertise, but that doesn't need to come from the analytic team. The data scientists, however, do need to know how to work with SMEs to extract the needed knowledge in the most effective way.

Chapter Nuggets

- Launching into data analytics without professional assistance often leads to trouble. Even companies with considerable experience in the field usually require ongoing professional support with the hard science.
- When you're hiring consultants, it can be difficult to wade through the hype. Many consulting companies, especially those that offer business intelligence (BI) services, may accept higher-level analytics engagements in hopes that they can muddle their way through.

- In most cases, it's not necessary, or even particularly helpful, for analytics consultants to have experience in your specific industry, as long as they are proven experts in solving data analysis problems.
- Subject-matter experts (SMEs) need to be on call for the analytics team, but their commitment level is usually modest and affordable.

CHAPTER 7

UNDERSTANDING THE DATA MINING PROCESS

To succeed as a leader of analytics projects, you need to understand the data mining process. A data analytics initiative is much like a research project. The data scientist embarks on a series of "test and learn"[16] steps with a general goal in mind, but without clearly knowing what the ultimate results will be. It's an iterative process in which the lessons learned at each step trigger new and increasingly focused questions that can lead to a re-examination and re-execution of prior steps.

Early practitioners of data mining developed their own approaches as they went along. Since they didn't have the benefit of a standardized approach, only the most experienced produced reliable and repeatable results. Consequently, it was harder to demonstrate to potential clients that data science was sufficiently mature as a profession to merit their trust.

In the late 1990s, some industry pioneers responded to the need for a more stable and tool-agnostic data mining methodology by developing CRISP-DM (an acronym for Cross-Industry Standard Process for Data Mining). Today, most competent data miners follow this model. Because it is so widely used, you will find it helpful to be familiar with it. In this chapter we will use it as a framework for discussing the data mining process.

The CRISP-DM Process

CRISP-DM identifies six phases through which all data mining projects progress. As depicted in Figure 7-1, they are: (1) business understanding, (2) data understanding, (3) data preparation, (4) modeling, (5) evaluation, and (6) deployment. In the illustration, the clockwise arrows indicate the most common path of progression. However, because the process is iterative, the workflow may circulate back and forth between different phases. For example, the arrow extending from data understanding to business understanding indicates how learning about the data can reveal gaps in understanding the business. These gaps must be addressed before the project can move forward to data preparation.

---

16 We first heard this term at a Predictive Analytics World conference used by Dean Silverman, a former IRS executive who headed the Office of Compliance Analytics.

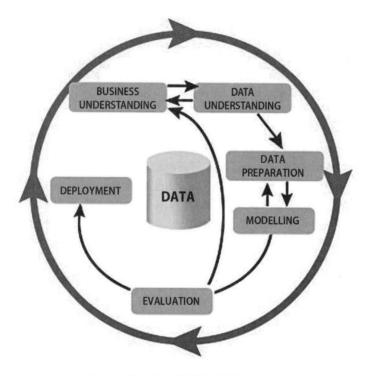

Figure 7-1: The CRISP-DM Process

The outer circle in Figure 7-1 illustrates how the constantly changing world environment can impact a model's performance. Dr. John Elder, the founder of our firm, first experienced this phenomenon when he developed a financial model that identified an area of inefficiency in the stock market. For a decade, John and his client made investments based on this information and earned a high rate of return. Gradually, however, the model's "edge" dulled, as others discovered and exploited this "pocket of inefficiency" in the market.

When the terrorist attack occurred in New York City on September 11, 2001, John and his client expected the models to stop working completely, since the world on which it had been trained had arguably changed. They temporarily ceased their investment activity, yet monitored how it would have performed. Surprisingly, the models continued to perform reasonably well for months, but within a year the results deteriorated. It seems it took participants in the stock market about a year to adjust fully to the new reality, so the lessons learned from patterns of yesteryear were no longer useful.[17]

The housing crisis of 2008-2009 presents another example of how changes in the outside world can affect the design and operation of a model. All major credit card companies use predictive analytics to assess the credit-worthiness of potential customers. When designing these models prior to 2008, data scientists often included late mortgage payments as one of the key negative factors. Applicants who paid their mortgages on time had a better chance of getting a credit card.

During the housing crisis, however, it turned out that many people chose to pay their credit cards before they paid their mortgages. In other words, there was little or no correlation between late mortgage payments and late credit card payments. In some cases, there was even an inverse correlation, perhaps caused by consumers' evaluation of the changing downside risks of the two types of debt default. Data scientists had to recognize this new reality and adjust their credit evaluation models to best predict default.

These examples illustrate why it is necessary to periodically back-test (monitor) the results of models to see whether their predictions are still accurate. For example, monitoring a model that predicts the price of a stock is easy: you just need to wait for a period of time and check the actual price of the stock against the prediction. In contrast, monitoring a model that predicts fraud is difficult, because of the difficulty of getting accurately labeled cases. Years of investigation and adjudication are typically required to prove that fraud does exist, assuming a prosecutor is even willing to accept the case.

Resist the Temptation to Take Shortcuts

Analytic teams must have sufficient knowledge and experience with the business and with the data in order to build a properly qualified model. Taking shortcuts and making assumptions about the meaning of data elements based on their names or labels, instead of digging into data dictionaries and asking SMEs, can lead to costly mistakes.

---

17 Eric Siegel relates other details of this story as the motivating real-world story for the power of Analytics in Chapter 1 of his excellent book *Predictive Analytics: The Power to Predict Who Will Click, Buy, Lie, or Die.*

In almost every data mining engagement we have conducted, management has put subtle but firm pressure on us to shortcut the process of business and data understanding. We empathize with our clients' desires for fast results, and it would be easy to yield to this pressure. It takes time and effort to consult SMEs and think through the business questions driving the analysis. We resist taking shortcuts, because we know from experience that success comes from understanding the business before attempting to fit the model. Analytical methods applied in a vacuum without the benefit of subject-matter knowledge can produce models that are technically accurate, but the insights or predictions these models produce will likely be useless to the business.

At the heart of every data mining success you will find someone who has taken the time to skillfully manage communication between groups with different knowledge sets and lexicons. There is no "magic" in the mathematics of fitting models, but there is some art in managing the communication path between business experts and analytic professionals. Before the data scientists begin fitting models and generating analytical results, they should have a competent understanding of the subject matter the model will process. At an early stage, they should evaluate the knowledge the business is transferring to them to ensure it is relevant, accurate, and complete.

A data analytics project is more likely to succeed when business subject-matter experts contribute to the definition, understanding, and qualification of the analytic model throughout the model-building process (see Figure 7-2). As they work with the data scientists, they will gain a better understanding of analytic methods, which in turn will give them a higher level of confidence in the model results. A mutually supportive communication channel that connects the knowledge sets and lexicons of SMEs with the model-building expertise of data scientists can produce magical results!

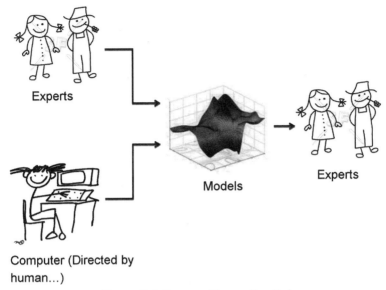

Experts

Models

Experts

Computer (Directed by human...)

Figure 7-2: Experts Have a Key Role

Up to this point, we've presented a fairly high-level overview of the data science field and what it takes to start and manage an analytics program. In the next several chapters, our explanations of the actual data mining process get a little more technical. Stick with us, and you'll gain a deeper understanding of the analytic process from the data scientist's perspective. This knowledge will be helpful to you as you interface with data scientists and help manage data analytics initiatives.

Chapter Nuggets

- A data analytics initiative is like a research project. The data scientist embarks on a series of "test and learn" steps with a general goal, but without knowing what the ultimate results will be. It's an iterative process. Lessons learned at each step can trigger new and increasingly focused questions that can lead to a re-examination and re-execution of prior steps.
- It is necessary to periodically back-test the results of models to see whether their predictions are still accurate.
- Analytic professionals must have access to people with knowledge and experience with the business and with the data in order for the team to build a properly qualified model.
- Taking shortcuts and making assumptions about the meaning of data elements based on their names or labels, instead of digging

into data dictionaries or asking subject-matter experts, can lead to costly mistakes.

- At the heart of every data mining success you will find someone who has taken the time to skillfully manage communication between groups with different knowledge sets and lexicons.
- A data analytics project is much more likely to succeed when business subject-matter experts contribute to the definition, understanding, and qualification of the analytic model throughout the model-building process.

CHAPTER 8

UNDERSTANDING THE BUSINESS

Of the six phases of the CRISP-DM process discussed in the previous chapter, we consider business understanding to be the most crucial. This phase entails understanding the organization's business objectives and requirements, converting this knowledge into a definition of a problem, and developing a preliminary plan to solve that problem. In order to construct a successful model, the data scientist must understand how the business functions and how it will use the data. Even the most technologically advanced data mining model will produce trivial and possibly misleading results if it is disconnected from the purposes and goals of the business.

An important aspect of this phase is defining how the model will impact the workflow and decision-making processes of the business. To achieve maximum return on the investment in analytics, the results of the initiative must lead to advantageous changes in business operations.

Different constituencies within an organization typically want different information from a model. For example, the marketing group might want to know which products and geographic areas merit more promotional support; the customer service department might want to know which customers represent the highest risk for attrition; the financial department may be interested in knowing which customers are credit risks; and individual sales reps might want to know which customers have the biggest potential for future purchases.

Connecting the business objectives to the input data usually requires considerable time and effort. The data scientist must interview subject-matter experts within the company to determine the objectives of the project, the resources available (people, data, and technology), the precise definitions of terms to be used, the projected costs and benefits of the project, and the projected return on investment (ROI).

Many companies can't understand why so much time must be spent on understanding the business. They seem to think the data scientist should just be able to take their data, put it in a magic "analytical model" box, turn the crank, and churn out the desired information. We call this the "black box fallacy." A data scientist who tries to build an analytic model without consulting SMEs is like a lawyer who tries to handle a case without consulting the client.

Clarifying Your Objective

Take sufficient time and care to clarify the purpose of your data analytics initiative. If you don't get your objective right, your whole project can be a waste of time and money.

A team of our data scientists recently spent more than eight hours on the phone with several business and technical people who work at the home office of one of our clients. This provider of outpatient medical services needed to predict the rate at which subscribers were likely to be referred out of their network. They needed this information to set up adequate cash reserves against the lost revenues. Reserving too much money would unnecessarily restrict their working capital, and reserving too little would expose them to financial and legal risks. The purpose of this effort was to refine this original business question: "How many people will be referred out of our network?"

Our first question during the call was, "What does 'referred out' mean?" After considerable discussion, the company decided to apply the term only to patients who left the network for non-emergency reasons.

Next, we needed to know what timeframe the model should cover. Should it predict the number of referrals expected in the next week, the next month, the next quarter, or the next year? The answer would affect model design, data preparation, and many other aspects of the analytical process. After much discussion, we agreed that a timeframe of twelve months would be best for business purposes.

We then deliberated about what population of people our model should include. For example, did the company want to include all who were eligible for its programs, or only those who had recently received services? After discussion, the client decided to include only patients who had received services in the past twenty-four months.

Next, we discussed how to measure the success of the model. After considering various options, we agreed to measure success based on how closely the model's predictions tracked actual referral costs.

It took us a full day on the phone to settle these questions, and that was only one conversation among many. There's just no shortcut around this phase of the process. A model built on a poor understanding of the business will likely deliver disappointing results.

Unfortunately, against our recommendation, this client rushed into the data understanding phase without fully completing the business understanding phase. Months later, during the model validation phase, the project team struggled to arrive at a stopping point for model accuracy. When one member realized that they had shortcut the business understanding phase, the team went back and defined how the model would be put into use by the business. It then became clear to them that they had wasted considerable time refining the model, because the extra accuracy obtained in the recent months of modeling was not germane to the ultimate business use of the model. The client team learned a hard lesson, but one that proved valuable on subsequent projects.

BRYAN'S STORY

Part 5: Understanding the Business

Throughout the process, I played a vital role in helping the data scientists understand our business. Just as I had to explain the value of analytics to our business people, I had to explain our agency's culture and decision-making processes to the analytics people. They needed to understand how the government works before they could develop a realistic plan about how we should proceed. Our partnership really started to take hold when the data mining people began to understand our business.

Working with data permitted us to ask deeper questions. For example, we could ask, "Why is this happening? How can we prevent that from happening?" Asking these deeper questions caused us to evolve as an organization.

Defining the Terminology

Precise goal definitions are essential for proper business understanding. A motion picture studio once asked a colleague of ours to develop a model to predict the most probable date and location of peak leaf color. Setting up to shoot a movie on location is expensive, so predicting the best filming conditions could potentially save the studio many thousands of dollars.

As our colleague interviewed this client to ensure that he clearly understood the business goal of the model, he discovered that the studio didn't really want to know the most probable date that leaves would attain maximum color, as defined scientifically. The studio actually wanted to know the most probable *sunny* day when leaves would attain the greatest *diversity* of color. In modeling, such distinctions can make a big difference. Our colleague persevered in understanding the precise project goal, so he wouldn't waste effort solving the wrong and very difficult problem.

An executive with a Texas-based oil and gas producer asked us to help him reduce the number of operational shutdowns the company was experiencing with its Wyoming wells. From internal company reports, this executive had learned that these work stoppages were due to "freeze" problems. He asked us to build a model that would predict when and where production wells were most likely to "freeze," so the company could take preventative action.

As our data scientists began working on the project, they noticed that the data coming in didn't match the problem the executive had described. Upon investigation, they found that the people in the field were working with a different definition of "freeze." They were using the term to describe a well stoppage primarily due to cold weather, while the executive had thought the term applied to stoppages for *any* reason, including planned maintenance! We eventually straightened out the team's mutual misunderstanding and developed the model using the narrower definition.

In designing a data mining project, it's often advantageous to narrow the scope. For example, instead of addressing a problem on a national level, one of our clients decided to focus initially on two regions. Management deliberately chose regions with very different characteristics, to provide the maximum amount of information. Once the model is designed for these regions, the company may apply it to a wider geographical area.

Framing the Questions

At the beginning of a data analytics project, devote careful attention to formulating the business questions the model is to answer. Aim your analytic weapon carefully! Data analytics requires a willingness to accept a level of uncertainty by letting go of preconceived notions and unsubstantiated assumptions. Properly framed questions can enable a model to uncover new, deeper insights that no one previously thought to seek.

Data analytics clearly demonstrated its power by revealing unexpected answers to problems during a meeting we had with a VP of customer service for a major corporation. This VP had asked her internal audit team to explain a recent increase in customer complaints. The head of the audit team had shared her team's data with us and invited us to attend the meeting.

The audit leader opened the meeting by reporting, "Your customer complaints are up this year."

"Yes, I know," said the VP of customer service.

"Most of them relate to delivery," the audit team leader added.

"I already know that," said the VP of customer service.

"And most of those are centered around your highest volume product," continued the head of the audit team.

"I know that, too," said the VP of customer service. Somewhat exasperated, she turned and asked us, "Do you have anything to add from your analysis?"

"Yes," we said. "The data indicates that three new electronic channels have been opened, so you're now getting feedback from your customers through email, Twitter, and websites. We hypothesize that the higher number of complaints is due not to poorer quality, but simply to more and better avenues for receiving customer feedback."

The VP breathed a sigh of relief. She, of course, knew that the corporation had made it easier for customers to provide feedback, but she had not thought to make the connection between this policy change and the higher level of complaints. We only made the connection because the data revealed it to us. Our data analysis precipitated a paradigm shift in thinking that ordinary reports failed to expose.

As human beings and managers, we typically strive to specify the exact questions we want answered or the exact problems we want solved. In this case, we could have tried to build the model to answer the question, "How can we reduce customer complaints?" However, in data analytics, overly specific presuppositions can impair results. So, we built the model around the question, "How do we better classify these customer complaints and address them?" This narrowly focused question enabled the model to uncover useful insights. As is often true with data analytics, the data revealed something completely unexpected. Complaints were up because of a change in processes, not because of an increase in problems. It was actually good news, not bad!

Understanding the business takes time, but in our opinion it is the most crucial step in data analytics!

An Unexpected Finding

For several years, our firm worked with a large, nationally recognized computer retailer. Our first project was to help identify service providers who were seeking to be reimbursed for computer repair services they didn't actually perform. This fraud-detection project was very successful—it quickly saved many millions of dollars—and the client expanded its work with us into new areas.

As our working relationship matured, one day the company handed us some data that had confounded them for a long time. They were puzzled and disturbed by the large number of warranty returns their service-provider customers were submitting without any identification of the problems. These unexplained returns were more expensive than normal returns because our client's technicians had to put in extra time trying to diagnose the issues. In the great majority of cases, the technicians could find no fault with these returned computers, so they labeled them "NFF" (no fault found). Nevertheless, since the computers were under warranty, our client had to ship brand new computers or parts to the service providers who returned the "defective" ones.

At this point, our data scientists were well-acquainted with our client's business, and they eagerly dug into this data. Much to everyone's surprise, intensive data analytics analysis revealed that a large number of the NFF returns were coming from two large international companies, and that almost all of the returns occurred just before the warranties expired on that equipment.

It then became clear that these two large international companies were abusing our client's generous warranty policy by habitually returning computers with fictitious complaints simply to get new ones. Because of this unethical practice, our client was wasting considerable sums of money replacing perfectly good equipment. Payments to technicians for unnecessary repairs and costs associated with excessively high used-equipment inventory exacerbated the burden. This finding shocked our client because management had previously considered these two service providers to be among their best customers. We weren't privy to details, but we understand that some dramatic, high-level conversations took place between our client and those two large service providers.

This story is a good example of two important issues related to data science. First, it illustrates how a solid business understanding leads to better results. Second, it reveals how brand new findings, not hypothesized by an expert, can be discovered deep in data by data scientists who know what questions to ask and how to look for answers.

Our team uncovered this previously unknown pattern on the "no fault found" problem because we were already intimately familiar with the client's business processes and data. It was actually through our combined knowl-edge from two different projects—the NFF problem and the service-provider fraud project—that we discovered how these two large companies were taking advantage of the client's generous warranty program. In our multiple years working with this computer retailer, several such successes have resulted in the recovery and documentation of tens of millions of dollars.

Chapter Nuggets

- Business understanding is the most crucial of the six phases of the CRISP-DM process.
- A successful model requires that the data scientists understand how the business functions and how it will use the data. If disconnected from the purposes and goals of the business, even the most advanced model will produce trivial or misleading results.
- At the beginning of a data analytics project, carefully formulate the business questions the model is to answer. Avoid making them too general or too specific.

CHAPTER 9

UNDERSTANDING AND PREPARING THE DATA

Data scientists who build analytical models that mine data and come up with interesting insights are quite the rage these days. Dr. Thomas Davenport, a respected authority and widely read author on the subject of data analytics, has called data science "the sexiest job of the 21st century,"[18] but few people consider the data sexy! Data is often messy, and it's so abundant that we sometimes feel as if we're drowning in it.

To an analytics expert, though, data represents a treasure trove of information. Without it, the analytical models can't function. Raw data itself has little analytical value until it's properly understood and prepared.

After gaining a basic understanding of the business, the data scientist moves on to understanding the data and preparing the data for modeling. The entire process of data mining is iterative, and these two phases are especially so. Preparation of the data often leads to further understanding of the data, which in turn may spur further feature engineering.

"Wrangling" the data can be the most time-consuming part of the process, with the possible exception of the implementation of the model. Larger organizations deal with huge data sets composed of tens of millions of cases. Each data set can have hundreds of fields, some with cryptic names and meanings. Data derived from a variety of sources may be in different formats that must be restructured for compatibility and then joined together. Before it can be addressed by data mining algorithms, unstructured data, such as text, may require many stages of filtering and transforming to map it into structured forms. Creative, quality work is required at this stage to lay the groundwork for modeling success.

Understanding the Data

Until companies get into data analytics and understand its benefits, most regard data as more of a burden than an asset. They often store it in discrete

---

18 Dr. Davenport is the President's Distinguished Professor in Information Technology and Management at Babson College, a research fellow at the MIT Center for Digital Business, and a senior advisor to Deloitte Analytics. This quote appeared in an article he wrote for the October 2012 issue of the *Harvard Business Review*.

compartments to satisfy record-keeping requirements, with little consideration for how it might be used for analytic model building. For example, sales-order information may be disconnected from customer information, with neither linked to product information. Consequently, the data scientist must usually spend considerable time gathering, joining, and preparing the data for the purpose of analytics.

During the preparation phase, data scientists will need to engage in hours of conversation with subject-matter experts within the organization to understand the meaning and relevance of each data element. Using this information, they can compile data dictionaries that explain where each feature (column of data) originates, how it's generated, its meaning, and how it impacts the business. Even when data scientists come into a project with some knowledge of the data, they still must thoroughly test these understandings before building a model. Big problems can result if the data scientist makes incorrect assumptions about the meanings or names of data elements.

In most organizations, users or caretakers of the data only understand the chunks of the database that relate to their specific job responsibilities. In a transportation database, for example, one employee might understand the aspects relating to contracts, another might understand the fields relating to routing, and still another might understand the data pertaining to fuel usage. The data scientist must understand the entire data set and take all of its dimensions into account when building the analytical model.

Cleaning the Data

Any data set, of even modest size, is going to have problems. Some of the data will be missing, corrupted, or poorly organized. There will be records that contain unexpected or missing values, and some data that is intended to have the same meaning will be represented inconsistently (e.g., "Street" might also be written as "St.").

It's not necessary to completely clean up data before turning it over, however. We urge our clients to provide us with their data regardless of condition, and then we can help them decide what to do next. Competent data scientists are accustomed to working with messy data, and they have tools and techniques to get around the most challenging data problems. Hesitation in getting data to the data scientist is a major cause—perhaps *the* major cause—of project delays.

One federal agency that called us in for a data mining engagement had a very difficult time turning over its data. In every weekly meeting, management told us they were "getting the data together." After nine months of waiting for the perfect data, they had to issue a contract modification to extend the period of performance. Several months later, another contract extension was needed, and then another. For reasons unknown to us, they kept feeling that their data was not good enough. It took us almost 2½ years to complete the project; understandably, the costs were higher than originally planned. If they had been willing to share their original data set with us, we could have completed the project in just a few months.

On a more positive note, another of our clients—a large, multinational corporation—acknowledged from the beginning that some data elements were missing values, and that some records were inconsistent. Nevertheless, management went ahead and provided us with a sample data set. Two of our data scientists analyzed it, and in less than a day we identified segments of the data that were good enough to begin the project.

"Perfect" Data

To be useful, data must be available in the right form and the right volume, but that doesn't mean it has to be perfect. Companies that insist on trying to perfect their data before turning it over usually end up unnecessarily delaying their projects and increasing their costs.

On the other hand, organizations that think their data is already perfect often get upset when we don't immediately start using it. Even when a data set is relatively clean, the data scientists must spend considerable time understanding it and ensuring that it is properly prepared for the modeling process.

When our firm presented a project plan to a healthcare services company, the organization's leaders pushed back hard on the schedule. "We've provided you with extremely clean data," they argued. "Why are you planning to spend so much time on data preparation?"

After some difficult conversations, our firm commenced the engagement, being careful not to rush the data-understanding and the data-preparation processes. In the course of the assignment, we found some significant problems in the data and reported them to management. For example, some customer documents had multiple ship dates, sometimes months apart, and others had ship dates that preceded the order dates. Management reluctantly acknowledged that the data needed to be cleaned before the modeling process could begin, and they agreed to a more reasonable schedule.

In another case, the management of a large petrochemical company asked us to build a model to analyze how some of their field "interventions" (i.e., actions to correct problems or increase production) were affecting their business operations. At the beginning of the project they gave us terabytes of data, which they believed were clean and complete. Our team spent two weeks examining the data and concluded that it was so messy that it was almost unusable. For instance, we discovered that the key target variable—interventions on gas wells—was totally missing.

The client shut the project down for eight weeks to deliberate about whether to continue. Meanwhile, our people found some clever ways around the problem of missing values by imputing likely values from other available data, where possible. When we explained our ideas, the client decided to proceed. Even though the additional costs incurred to clean up the data pushed the project over the original budget, it still generated a very high return on investment.

BRYAN'S STORY
Part 6: Understanding and Preparing the Data

Throughout the modeling process, I felt like I was in the middle of a tug-of-war between the data scientists and the chief information officer.

"Give us all of your data so we can play with it," the data scientists would say.

"We'll give you the data. Just tell us exactly what you want and where you want us to put it," the CIO would reply.

"We don't know what we want until we see what you have," the analytics people would respond.

Back and forth it went. The data scientists wanted unencumbered access, and the CIO's traditional stance was to lock up data so no one could get to it. I finally broke the deadlock by suggesting that we put a very small amount of the data set in a secure area, so the data scientists could play around with it. When they had the ability to experiment, they came up with some ideas that we developed into a model.

Collecting and Preparing the Data

Once the data is understood, it must be collected and prepared for the modeling process. Some of the data will be used to build the model, and a sample of the data will held out to validate the model. We'll discuss this validation process and the use of this hold-out data in Chapter 11.

We believe that data scientists will almost never be able to simply walk in the door, take the data from the client, and begin a successful modeling process. They first need to build data dictionaries and talk with the data experts in the organization to understand what the data fields represent. Even if the organization has well-structured data, the data scientists will still need to spend considerable time preparing it to create models of high quality.

Recently a client hired us to take over an assignment that a very large, high-priced data analytics firm had failed to complete satisfactorily after two people-years of effort. Our data scientists began the engagement in our firm's usual manner by framing the questions to be answered, and understanding and preparing the data. After a few days, one of the company's managers complained, "Why are you spending so much time on this preliminary work? The other firm we hired took the data from us and immediately started building the models."

"That's probably why the other firm's models failed to produce the desired results," we explained. Subsequently, we found flaws in the data, which identified internal processes that needed correcting. We also became aware of many fields that were different from their surface meaning, and we discovered some very useful feature transformations. The models we built upon this solid foundation were extremely useful to the organization.

Data scientists need timely access to the full complement of data required for modeling. Some organizations supply incomplete sets of data or data sets without dictionaries. Others fail to provide information about how the data was collected, what the data fields mean, how the data is maintained, how it is used, and why it is messy or incomplete.

Some data owners within organizations behave like wary guard dogs. No amount of explaining, reassuring, or cajoling can get them to relax their grip on the data.

What's the reason for this overly protective attitude? Frankly, some database administrators, analysts, and program executives are afraid of what analysis of the data will reveal. Other data owners may think they can do the analytics job better themselves, and they resent the intrusion of outsiders into their domain. Regardless of the reasons, the bottom line is that one person withholding key data can stop a data analytics project dead in its tracks.

Fostering Cooperation

To promote buy-in and cooperation on your data mining project, invite data owners to participate in the formative stages. They will have a stronger desire to see the project succeed if you welcome and value their input from the beginning.

One of our clients, a moderate-size financial services firm, learned the hard way about the importance of gaining buy-in. Almost immediately after we started our engagement, the company held a two-day kickoff event with business executives, subject-matter experts, and internal analysts. The analyst who would be providing the data to us had had dreams of doing the work himself, and he quickly made our firm the target of his hostility. He openly challenged almost every idea presented by our data scientists and the other members of the client company's team.

From a technical perspective, the project was rather straightforward and could have been an easy success for everyone. Within two weeks, however, it became clear that the engagement was doomed. Tired of the constant pushback from their junior technologist, management cancelled it. Had the data keeper been on board initially, he and his colleagues could have become stars from the quick successes that were possible. Instead, the data analytics initiative went nowhere. Thousands of dollars went down the drain, and far more importantly, hundreds of thousands of dollars of likely gain were left unclaimed.

Such overt and direct opposition is actually rare; more often, obstructers passive-aggressively create an environment where data are always being "worked on" and deliveries are slow-rolled until the project dies of weariness before analysis ever really starts. Beware when the keepers of the data want to delay the commencement of work until the data is "perfect" and completely defined. Great progress can be made with data samples, even as the more complete set of data is being dusted off for use.

Governing the Data

When an organization begins to appreciate the value of predictive analytics, it experiences a change in cultural attitude. People stop thinking of data as a costly nuisance that is useful only for documenting historical events and fulfilling statutory requirements. They begin to regard it as an asset with tremendous decision-making value. They stop thinking merely about how to warehouse data, and they start focusing on how to strategically acquire and utilize it. Data becomes as valuable to them as their human resources, technological expertise, facilities, and other assets that drive their business. They understand the importance of developing a data governance plan, which ensures that their data is accessible and in suitable form for making decisions.

Data governance plans that deal only with how data is stored in a warehouse can do more harm than good. Without a clear plan for how the data will be used, the company may find itself creating and storing data that is inaccurate and unhelpful. Dr. Peter Aiken[19] calls this type of data "ROT" (Redundant, Obsolete, and Trivial).

In many companies, the chief information officer (CIO) or the chief data officer (CDO) handles the data governance function. These "data czars" can be extremely helpful if their major goal is to strategically transform record-keeping data into analytically useful data. However, if they see their primary responsibility as safeguarding data, they can be an enormous obstacle to analytic success.

It's unreasonable to expect a CIO, CDO, or any other single person to have a comprehensive understanding of all an organization's data. Typically, multiple people within the organization will need to serve as data resources. Often, they may have different interpretations of the same data elements, which the data scientist must reconcile. It's common for different groups touching data to meet for the first time while working on a data analysis project, and this can have positive overall consequences for data governance at the firm.

Many organizations hire data management consultants to help them develop data governance plans. These consultants interface with the analytical model builders to determine how the data should be organized and stored to meet future analytical needs, just as the model builders consult with the intended users of the analytical output when building the model.

Preparing data is far from a glamorous job. It's akin to the scraping, sanding, and patching that one must do to prepare a room for painting. People rarely say, "What a beautifully prepared room!" However, a well-prepared room is easier to paint, and the result looks better and lasts longer. It's the same with data. An analytics project cannot succeed without good data. Its proper preparation speeds up the modeling process and produces better results.

---

19 Our friend, Dr. Aiken, serves as the founding director of the data consulting firm Data Blueprint. He is an associate professor of information systems at Virginia Commonwealth University, president of the International Data Management Association (DAMA), and the author of *The Case for the Chief Data Officer: Recasting the C-Suite to Leverage Your Most Valuable Asset*. He is widely recognized as one of the top ten data management authorities in the world.

Chapter Nuggets

- Preparing the data often leads to better understanding of the data, which in turn may provoke further feature transformation.
- Even when data scientists come into a project with some knowledge of the data, they still must thoroughly test their understandings before building a model. Don't assume that data labels alone reveal the meanings of data features.
- Any data set of even modest size will have problems.
- Competent data scientists know how to work with messy data, and they have tools and techniques to get around most data problems.
- Hesitation in getting data to the data scientist is perhaps *the* major cause of project delays.
- Data scientists use some of the data to build the model, and they hold out a sample to validate the model.
- Data scientists are rarely able to simply receive the data from the client, and begin the modeling process. They first need to build data dictionaries and talk with data experts in the organization to understand what the data fields represent.
- The analytics effort will suffer or fail if one or more data owners within the organization behave like a wary guard dog who cannot be persuaded to relax its grip on the data.
- To promote buy-in and cooperation on your data mining project, invite data owners to participate in its formative stages.
- An analytics project vitally depends on good data. Its proper preparation speeds up the modeling process and produces better results.

CHAPTER 10

BUILDING THE MODEL

In this chapter we will go into some detail about the design of models and the advantages and disadvantages of the different types of models. You should find this information very helpful if you are responsible for staffing or managing a data analytics project. You will do a better job as a manager if you can ask data scientists questions like the following:

- *Do you think an inductive or deductive model would be better for my application?*
- *How many different modeling techniques are we capable of using?*
- *Why did you choose this particular type of model?*
- *Have you considered model ensembles?*
- *Can I see a distribution of results, and what was the variance?*
- *How will this model hold up on completely new data?*
- *How often should we back-test the model to ensure it's still producing accurate results?*

Just as students must spend may hours preparing for a tough one-hour exam, data scientists must spend considerable time preparing to build a model. On average, they spend 65-80 percent of their time understanding the business, and understanding and preparing the data, and only 20-35 percent on building and validating the model. (These estimates do not include the potentially considerable time required to deploy the model, which we'll discuss in Chapter 12.)

In the model-building phase, the data scientists select and apply modeling techniques and fit (or optimize) their parameters. This phase is something of a trial-and-error process, even though some of the statistical steps are closed-form (optimal) for specific assumptions. The data scientists will try an idea and test it. If it works, they will build on that success. If not, they will go back and try something else.

Inside the "Black Box"

Some people think of data analytics models as "black boxes," but when you're leading an analytics project, it's very helpful to know the strengths and weaknesses of what's inside the box. So, what exactly is a model? How can you tell if it's any good? In this chapter, we'll highlight answers to these questions.

This information will enable you to do a better job of hiring and working with data scientists. You will be able to ask better questions and make better decisions as a manager of a data analytics project when you understand what's involved, what's possible, and what the trade-offs are between the various approaches.

There is no single best way to build an analytical model. Many different approaches are possible, and skilled data scientists will have the knowledge and experience to know which ones best address a particular need. Data scientists who are knowledgeable about only one or two methods, such as linear regression or standard statistical analysis, will naturally tend to use those tools even when they won't achieve the best solution. The most successful data scientists understand how to use a variety of modeling techniques and they have the breadth of knowledge to evaluate their trade-offs.

When building a model, data scientists seek to develop an equation or set of rules to best fit the historical data, with the aim of using the model to draw inferences about future events. Model-building is an iterative process of exploration and optimization. The scientists are constantly experimenting with different analytic techniques, data features, and optimization options in an attempt to increase model accuracy.

At every stage, further improvements in performance may be possible, but not always advisable. Beyond a certain point, the costs of making additional refinements to the model begin to outweigh the benefits derived from them (the law of diminishing returns). If the analyst is inexperienced at building reliable models, too much optimization can lead to "overfit." Overfit occurs when the model "memorizes" the training data so thoroughly that it is unable to generalize well to new data. The ability to generalize to new data is the true measure of accuracy. Therefore, the goal of data scientists is not to obtain the best *technical* solution, but the best *practical* solution, keeping in mind the needs, constraints, and resources of the client.

Building an Illustrative Model

Suppose you own a credit card company, and you want to be able to predict the likelihood that new credit card applicants will default on their payments. You initially issued credit cards to nearly everyone who applied, but it turned out that a third of these new cardholders defaulted on their payments. Obviously, that's no way to run a business, so you decide to build a predictive analytics model. If your model can reasonably predict which applicants are creditworthy, you will save a lot of money.

Let's say that you have examined some past data and observed that credit card defaults are inversely correlated with an individual's credit rating and income level. In other words, defaults increase as credit scores and income levels decrease. You've also noticed a few other factors that tend to increase default rates, such as whether the applicant is a student, but you want to keep your model simple, so you decide to start by just considering credit scores and income levels.

In the interest of simplicity, you decide to build a linear regression model. That is the most popular approach for modeling the relationship between a dependent variable (y) and the explanatory variables (x). Regression methods assume there's a linear relationship between the predictors (explanatory variables) and your outcome. Because regression has a linear structure, we can express the model in the following mathematical equation:

$$y = \beta_0 + \beta_1 x_1 + \beta_2 x_2$$

If you are thinking that this looks like an equation for a straight line that you studied in high school trigonometry, congratulations! You didn't forget everything after all! Now, we only need to find values for the constants β_0, β_1, and β_2. Linear regression is a popular technique for this purpose because it allows one to find, mathematically, the ideal parameter values simultaneously and instantly (when "ideal" is defined as those values that minimize total *squared* error over the training data).

In the equation above, y is the creditworthiness you are seeking to determine for each applicant (a more useful indicator or risk than external credit score alone), x_1 and x_2 are input variables, and β_0, β_1, and β_2 are the coefficients found by linear regression that minimize squared error in estimating y over all the known (training) cases. If the training data has $y = 1$ recorded for a good customer and $y = 0$ for a defaulting one, then higher values of our estimate of y indicate the most creditworthy applicants.

In a graph, the data would lie in a 3-dimensional space, where the longitude and latitude would correspond to x_1 and x_2, respectively, and the altitude to y. The linear equation estimating y would be the plane that best fits through all the points in space, as shown in Figure 10-1. Best fitting in this case means that the squared error of our estimates across all historical data is mathematically minimized. Any change in the position, orientation, or tilt of the best plane would increase the overall error of the estimates.

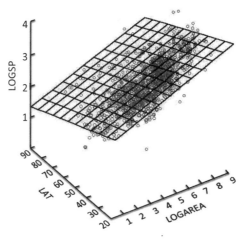

Figure 10-1: Estimation Surface of a 2-input Linear Regression Model

In the equation, the constant, β_0 is fit simultaneously with β_1 the coefficient for (e.g., credit score), and β_2 the coefficient for x_2 (e.g., income level).

Let's say that after studying the experiences of past customers, the model finds that a good credit score is twice as important as a high income level. If the two input variables have been scaled to have similar ranges, this means credit score information merits a weight two times the weight of income level information. Let's further assume the weight (parameter estimate) of credit score information was calculated to be 0.10, the weight (parameter estimate) of income level information was calculated to be 0.05, and the constant that works best with these weights is found to be 0.5.

With the three constants figured out, the equation is "fit" and becomes

$$y = .5 + .1x_1 + .05x_2.$$

For a particular credit card applicant, you'd fill the values for the inputs and get his or her score. For example, if an applicant's normalized value for credit score is 2 and for income is 3, then

$$y = .5 + .1\ (2) + .05\ (3)$$

$$y = .5 + .2 + .15$$

$$y = .85$$

If you had set a minimum threshold value of, say, .75, you would issue the card to this applicant.

Non-Linear Models

Because we are assuming a linear structure in the previous example, we know that the calculation to fit a plane to the data with minimum error will be fairly simple. With non-linear methods, on the other hand, rather than *assuming* a structure, we attempt to *discover* a structure that fits the data.

For example, Figure 10-2 reveals the equation for a neural network model that we built to rate home equity credit lines. The non-linear response surface of this model has seven input variables (x), five non-linear "hidden" nodes, and dozens of parameters (β). Consequently, it is much more complex and flexible than a LR model.

```
*************************************;
*** Begin Scoring Code for Neural;
*** Checking missing input Interval
*** ***************************;
IF NMISS(
IMP_CLAGE ,
IMP_DEBTINC ,
IMP_DELINQ ,
IMP_DEROG ,
IMP_MORTDUE ,
IMP_NINQ ,
IMP_YOJ ,
LOAN ) THEN DO;
SUBSTR(_WARN_, 1, 1) = 'M';
_DM_BAD = 1;
END;
*** ***********************.
*** Writing the Node intvl;
*** ***********************;
IF _DM_BAD EQ 0 THEN DO;
S_IMP_CLAGE = -2.13 + 0.012 * IMP_CLAGE;
S_IMP_DEBTINC = -1.68 + 0.063 * IMP_DEBTINC
;
S_IMP_DELINQ = -0.478 + 0.885 * IMP_DELINQ;
S_IMP_DEROG = -0.36 + 1.23* IMP_DEROG;
S_IMP_MORTDUE = -1.69 + 0.0000232 * IMP_MORTDUE
;
S_IMP_NINQ = -0.712 + 0.581 * IMP_NINQ;
S_IMP_YOJ = -1.22 + 0.135 * IMP_YOJ;
S_LOAN = -1.66031695856817 + 0.00008922612066 * LOAN;
END;
ELSE DO;
IF MISSING( IMP_CLAGE ) THEN S_IMP_CLAGE = .;
ELSE S_IMP_CLAGE = -2.13 + 0.0119 * IMP_CLAGE;
IF MISSING( IMP_DEBTINC ) THEN S_IMP_DEBTINC = .;
ELSE S_IMP_DEBTINC = -1.685 + 0.0633 *
IMP_DEBTINC;
IF MISSING( IMP_DELINQ ) THEN S_IMP_DELINQ = .;
ELSE S_IMP_DELINQ = -0.478+ 0.885*
IMP_DELINQ;
IF MISSING( IMP_DEROG ) THEN S_IMP_DEROG = .;
ELSE S_IMP_DEROG = -0.36+ 1.232 * IMP_DEROG;
IF MISSING( IMP_MORTDUE ) THEN S_IMP_MORTDUE = .;
ELSE S_IMP_MORTDUE = -1.69 + 0.0000232 *
IMP_MORTDUE;
IF MISSING( IMP_NINQ ) THEN S_IMP_NINQ = .;
ELSE S_IMP_NINQ = -0.712 + 0.581 * IMP_NINQ;
IF MISSING( IMP_YOJ ) THEN S_IMP_YOJ = .;
ELSE S_IMP_YOJ = -1.217+ 0.135 * IMP_YOJ;
IF MISSING( LOAN ) THEN S_LOAN = .;
ELSE S_LOAN = -1.66 + 0.000089 * LOAN;
END;
```

con't.

Figure 10-2: Non-linear Neural Network Model with Four Stages (1 of 2)

```
*** **************************.
*** Writing the Node bin, Node H1;
*** **************************.
IF _DM_BAD EQ 0 THEN DO;
 H11 = 1.279 * S_IMP_CLAGE + -1.88 *
 S_IMP_DEBTINC + -1.2477685671229 * S_IMP_DELINQ
 + -0.224 * S_IMP_DEROG + 1.778 *
 S_IMP_MORTDUE + -0.0192129643289 * S_IMP_NINQ
 + 0.159 * S_IMP_YOJ + 1.815* S_LOAN;
 H12 = -0.52 * S_IMP_CLAGE + -3.198 *
 S_IMP_DEBTINC + 1.3887599690037 * S_IMP_DELINQ
 + 0.586 * S_IMP_DEROG + -0.0206 *
 S_IMP_MORTDUE + 0.186 * S_IMP_NINQ
 + -0.307 * S_IMP_YOJ + -0.0504 * S_LOAN;
 H13 = -0.672 * S_IMP_CLAGE + 6.73 *
 S_IMP_DEBTINC + 0.50465577474013 * S_IMP_DELINQ
 + 0.625 * S_IMP_DEROG + 0.322 *
 S_IMP_MORTDUE + -0.237 * S_IMP_NINQ
 + 0.334 * S_IMP_YOJ + 0.184 * S_LOAN;
 H11 = H11 + 11.91 * M_DEBTINC0;
 H12 = H12 + 0.199 * M_DEBTINC0;
 H13 = H13 + -8.22 * M_DEBTINC0;
 H11 = -9.232 + H11;
 H12 = -4.49 + H12;
 H13 = -0.153 + H13;
 H11 = TANH(H11 );
 H12 = TANH(H12 );
 H13 = TANH(H13 );
END;
ELSE DO;
 H11 = .;
 H12 = .;
 H13 = .;
END;
*** **************************.
*** Writing the Node BAD;
*** **************************.
IF _DM_BAD EQ 0 THEN DO;
 P_BAD1 = -0.87 * H11 + 1.43 * H12
 + 3.74 * H13;
 P_BAD1 = 2.58 + P_BAD1;
 P_BAD0 = 0;
 _MAX_ = MAX (P_BAD1 , P_BAD0 );
 _SUM_ = 0.;
 P_BAD1 = EXP(P_BAD1 - _MAX_);
 _SUM_ = _SUM_ + P_BAD1;
 P_BAD0 = EXP(P_BAD0 - _MAX_);
 _SUM_ = _SUM_ + P_BAD0;
 P_BAD1 = P_BAD1 / _SUM_;
 P_BAD0 = P_BAD0 / _SUM_;
END;
ELSE DO;
 P_BAD1 = .;
 P_BAD0 = .;
END;
IF _DM_BAD EQ 1 THEN DO;
 P_BAD1 = 0.200;
 P_BAD0 = 0.800;
END;
```

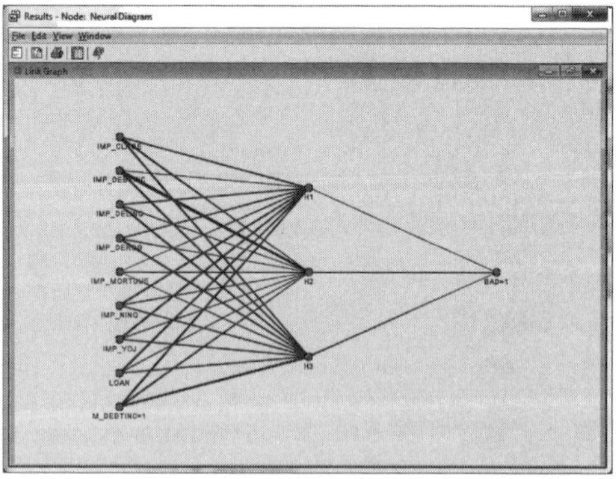

Figure 10-2: Non-linear Neural Network Model with Four Stages (2 of 2)

Unlike LR, the parameters aren't guaranteed to be the best fit. Non-linear techniques typically make multiple passes through the data searching for the best structure, which takes a lot of computer time. Therefore, non-linear algorithms contain trade-offs that ensure the algorithms can reach a stopping point. The necessary trade-offs that must be made while searching for the best structure sometimes lead to a stopping point that is not the optimal or best fit for the data. In many cases, however, even a sub-optimal non-linear model can outperform a linear one if the relationship between the predictors and target in the data is complex.

Choosing a Model

There are many different types of analytical models, each having particular strengths and weaknesses. The choice of model will depend on the type and quantity of the data, the goal of the data analytics project, the size of the budget, the availability of data analytics expertise, and other factors. No one model works best for every type of business problem. Some "data scientists" who are familiar with a certain type of model try to use it on every problem. That's a mistake!

Figure 10-3 depicts how five different types of models performed in tests our firm ran on six different types of data from the medical, financial, statistical, and signal processing fields. A higher score on the Y-axis indicates a higher relative error rate and therefore a poorer performance. (The worst of all out-of-sample error rates for each data set got a score near 1, and the best got a zero.)

Note how each model's effectiveness varies considerably depending on the nature of the data. For example, a projection pursuit regression model performed worst (with a high error rate) on the "German Credit" data, but it tied for second best (with a low error rate) on the (simulated) "Investment" problem. This illustrates why it's so important to try multiple types of models on your data.

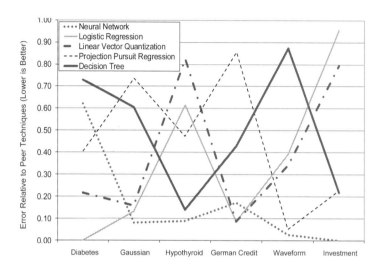

Figure 10-3: Comparing Relative Errors of Modeling Techniques[20]

Still, if data scientists use five or six different modeling techniques with, say, a hundred different elements, the model project can quickly get very complex. If the number of possible interactions among the data elements further increases, it is clear that data scientists cannot evaluate all possible combinations. They must be skilled at using machine learning and mathematics to find the best alternative models to try. As a purchaser of analytics services, be sure to ask the data scientists what models they have evaluated and what the results turned out to be. Sometimes they will favor one or two types of models and fail to consider others.

BRYAN'S STORY
Part 7: Building the Model

When the Elder people were building the model, some of the questions they asked us seemed kind of silly at times. I later realized that was due to our lack of understanding about what they were doing, but at the time, this caused some of our business people to get impatient and wonder if this analytics thing was going to work. My role was to try to reassure people and to be available to answer questions and interpret information as the model was being developed. This was probably the tensest part of the whole process. It required a lot of patience and faith in our data scientists.

---

20 Seni, Giovanni, and Elder, John. *Ensemble Methods in Data Mining: Improving Accuracy through Combining Predictions.* San Rafael, CA: Morgan & Claypool, 2010.

Response Surfaces of Predictive Models

The model in our linear regression example at the beginning of the chapter had only two variables (credit score and income level), so we could easily visualize it. Problems that involve more variables can only be expressed mathematically, especially when these variables are multiplied together or raised to higher powers (i.e., multiplied by themselves). All models, regardless of complexity, are just a mathematical equation that calculates a value for y given values of x. Figure 10-4 shows the response surfaces for five very different kinds of models. In order of increasing complexity, they are linear regression, decision tree, nearest neighbor, kernel density, and neural networks.

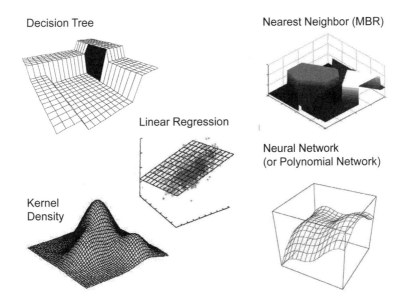

Decision Tree

Nearest Neighbor (MBR)

Linear Regression

Neural Network
(or Polynomial Network)

Kernel
Density

Figure 10-4: Response Surfaces of Leading Predictive Modeling Techniques[21]

The surfaces of these models represent the *predictions* of the value of y, not the actual data. Since the surfaces were defined to try to minimize errors, they represent answers (expected values) that are as close to known reality as practical. For instance, with the linear regression model in Figure 10-1, the values for x_1 and x_2 will establish a point on the plane where $y = 0$. If we then move up the y (vertical) axis to the response surface (grid), our model will give us our prediction.

---

21 This is a variation of Figure 18.3 on page 711 of the *Handbook of Statistical Analysis & Data Mining.*

The Trade-off between Accuracy and Interpretability

The linear regression model (Figure 10-1) was very simple. This gives it high interpretability. That is, if an applicant received a low score, we would only have to look at the two predictors (credit rating and income level) to understand why. We could have increased the accuracy of the model by including more variables, such as whether the applicant was a student, the number of other credit cards active, etc., but a greater number of variables increases the complexity of the model and reduces its interpretability. So, the increased accuracy may not merit the extra effort.

When it's important for management to understand why a model is producing certain results, data scientists may need to give up some accuracy to gain the desired interpretability. For instance, interpretability might be important in a model designed to detect vendors who are likely to commit waste, fraud, or abuse. If management understands not only which vendors present risks, but also what factors caused them to be flagged as higher risks, they can use this information to determine where to launch their investigations.

On the other hand, if we were building a model to predict stock market activity, the need for accuracy would almost certainly trump the desire for interpretability. This consideration, plus the complexity of the data, would cause us to favor an inductive model built from exploring the data, rather than a deductive model built via human expertise. Furthermore, since fundamental changes in the financial markets can dramatically affect the accuracy of our model, we should back-test it regularly so we can recognize and adjust to any significant changes in the marketplace and the data it produces.

Choosing and Testing Modeling Algorithms

By using a particular technique like regression, we introduce structure bias into the model. That is, we depend on the model to do the best it can to describe the data with its particular vocabulary. If we choose a Decision Tree, the model will be a piecewise landscape of disjointed constant levels, like a Manhattan skyline (Figure 10-4). Alternatively, a linear regression surface is a tilted plane, and a Kernel Density shape is like mounds of piled-up sand. Models that perform well on one shape generally do not perform as well on problems with a different shape. It's well worth the effort to try different model types to see which best describe the data.

Whatever model you choose, be sure to test it in as many ways as possible. Try fitting it on one set of data and evaluating it on another that has been unseen by the training or fitting algorithm. Then, store those results. It is best to do this repeatedly, changing which subset of the data (10 percent or so) is held out for evaluation. Good models produce distributions of evaluation results with a low variance, or spread. This is called "cross-validation," or "bootstrapping." It is the most effective way to evaluate models. If you perform only one test, you may get lucky or unlucky. Instead, you can more reliably measure quality by performing multiple tests and observing how the results vary.

Dealing with Variance

An inductive (machine learning) model will have greater variance than a deductive (human-designed) model. To explain the concept of variance, imagine two men who both wear a medium-size shirt. If one man loans his shirt to the other, it should fit quite nicely. In other words, there will not be much variance in the fit between the two men.

However, if the man loaning the shirt has had it tailored to his specific body shape, it almost certainly will not fit the second man as well. Put another way, the additional tailoring will have improved the fit of the shirt on the first man, but it will have increased the *variance* of fit between the two men.

In modeling, a deductive model is like a standard-size shirt, and an inductive model is like a tailored shirt. Since an inductive model is "tailored" by machine learning to a particular set of data, it will fit the data set better (i.e., have greater accuracy) than a deductive model. However, it could also have more misalignments (i.e., greater variance) than a deductive model when fit on a new set of similar data. In other words, the increased accuracy of the inductive model comes at the cost of greater variance.

It is helpful to understand the concept of variance when managing a data analytics project. For example, if a data scientist comes to you and says that his inductive model has achieved 98 percent accuracy, ask some questions before you get excited. Find out how many sets of data were used to test the model, and what the results were. If the scientist only tested the model on one or two sets of new data, it may exhibit a high degree of variance when exposed to new data. The results of such a model could lead to erroneous decisions. (Beware of inexperienced modelers who report only training performance and have no idea how a model will perform on new data!)

One test won't adequately measure the ultimate accuracy of any model. Models with low bias (i.e., machine learning models) require a distribution of results obtained by running dozens of tests, or more, on different samples of data.

Model Ensembles

Model ensembles employ multiple, diverse models to produce results that are typically more reliable and accurate than those of a single model. Ensembles also tend to reduce variance and protect against over-fit. As we have noted, over-fit occurs when an inductive model "over-learns" the historical data based on the known outcomes, so that it makes less stable and less accurate predictions on new data. While ensembles may seem dauntingly complex, they actually are less complex in behavior than single models[22]. Because they are less flexible in their adjustment to arbitrary changes in the data, they generalize to new data more accurately.

John Elder was a pioneer in the use of ensembles as a data analytics technique back in the 1990s. At the time, he called it "bundling" because it involved combining multiple diverse types of modeling algorithms. He first used this approach to classify six different species of bats, based on time-frequency characteristics of their sophisticated echolocation chirps. This classification problem was challenging because of its very small sample size, not to mention the difficulty of capturing the bats, classifying their species, releasing them to chirp, and reducing the background noise on the recordings. Thank goodness for graduate students!

Figure 10-5 refers to the same sets of data discussed earlier in connection with Figure 10-3, but this time we're using four different types of model ensembles. Notice that the accuracy of the models on all six sets of data has improved significantly. That is, the error rates for every type of ensemble tend to be much lower than those for individual models (Figure 10-3), and their variance (spread) is much lower as well.

The small lesson is that the fancier methods of ensembling, such as "Advisor Perceptrons," do somewhat better than the ordinary methods such as "Average" and "Vote."[23] However, the big news is that any of these

---

22 For a more detailed discussion on this subject, see Chapter 6 of; Seni, Giovanni, and Elder, John. *Ensemble Methods in Data Mining: Improving Accuracy through Combining Predictions.* San Rafael, CA: Morgan & Claypool, 2010. That chapter was originally a paper Dr. Elder was invited to present at the National Academy of Sciences.

23 Ibid

reasonable ensemble methods do better than individual modeling methods. (Perhaps the one exception on these data sets is that Neural Networks happened to do as well in our test as ensembles, but it was not clear ahead of time that this would be so, whereas all the ensemble methods performed very well.)

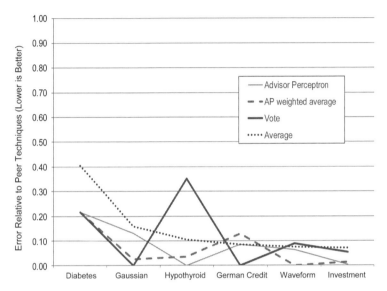

Figure 10-5: Error Comparison of Four Different Ensembles

The data mining field is complex and constantly changing, so this chapter has necessarily been limited in scope. For more comprehensive information on data modeling principles, we refer you to the *Handbook of Statistical Analysis and Data Mining Applications* by Nisbet, Elder, and Miner[24].

Chapter Nuggets

- When our firm is conducting a data analytics project, we typically spend 65-80 percent of our time on the preparatory phases of understanding the business and preparing the data. We spend only 20-35 percent of our time on building and validating the model. These estimates don't include the time required to deploy the model, which can be considerable.

---

24 Robert Nisbet, John Elder, and Gary Miner, *Handbook of Statistical Analysis and Data Mining Applications*, Academic Press, 2009)

- In the model-building phase, the data scientist selects and applies modeling techniques and calibrates their parameters to optimal values. It involves a mix of optimization and educated trial and error.

- Many different modeling approaches are possible, and a skilled data scientist must have the knowledge and experience to know which ones best address a particular need. Each has its strengths and weaknesses.

- Even when improvements in performance are possible, they may not be advisable. Beyond a certain point, the costs of making additional refinements to the model begin to outweigh the benefits derived from them (the law of diminishing returns). Therefore, the goal of data scientists is not to arrive at the best technical solution, but at the best practical solution, keeping in mind the needs, constraints, and resources of the client.

- The choice of model will depend on the type and quantity of the data, the goal of the data analytics project, the size of the budget, the availability of data analytics expertise, and other factors. No one model type will work for every type of business problem.

- Some people become familiar with a certain type of model and try to use it on every problem. That's a mistake!

- When it's important for management to understand why a model is producing certain results, data scientists may need to trade away some accuracy to gain the desired interpretability.

- Model ensembles employ multiple, diverse models to produce results that typically are more reliable than a single model. Ensembles also tend to reduce variance and protect against over-fit. While ensembles may seem dauntingly complex, they actually are less complex in behavior than single models. Because they are less flexible in their adjustment to arbitrary changes in the data, they generalize to new data more accurately.

CHAPTER 11

VALIDATING THE MODEL

Once the model is built and appears to be generating high-quality results on the training data, the data scientist must thoroughly validate it to ensure that it works on new data and that it properly considers all business issues and achieves all business objectives. Under-valuing the importance of validation can lead to serious problems later. The information in this chapter will help you be a much better manager of data analytics projects.

Validation has both a technical and a business aspect. Technical validation relates to how well the model performs on the data. Business validation relates to how well the model achieves its intended business purpose. Often a project will circle back and forth several times between validation and business understanding, before the model is ready for deployment.

Technical Validation

To be useful, the model must achieve a certain level of accuracy on new data that it will encounter "in the field." Technical validation seeks to answer the question, "Will the model give us accurate predictions when we feed it new samples of data that are similar in kind, but different in detail from the data we used to build it?"

The most common industry practice for measuring out-of-sample accuracy trains the model on a random subset of 70-80 percent of the data and tests it on the remaining 20-30 percent. Similar accuracy on the evaluation data compared to the training data is evidence that the model is not overfit. When the model is not tailored too finely to the specifics of the training data, it should perform approximately as well on new, live data as it did on the evaluation data.

As an aside, there are many different measures of model fit, though the most common are *squared error* for estimation problems and *misclassification rate* for classification problems. Squared error is rarely the measure that best corresponds to the trade-offs in the business problem; yet, it is usually employed due to convenience. The math works out so that solutions can be found very rapidly. Only a few modeling algorithms give you an alternative metric, like absolute error, and the good news is that squared error is not bad.

On the other hand, misclassification rate is not a good metric because it implies all errors are equally bad. When working with classification problems, it's much better to take into account the cost of different kinds of errors. The goal should be to minimize the overall *cost* of mistakes, not simply their *count*.

After two decades of experience, Elder Research has learned that one test (a single-point statistical measure) is not a reliable test of model fit. Our practice is to conduct dozens of training and evaluation runs, each time using a different randomized split of the original training data.

When validating models, we find it helpful to partition the data samples by dividing them into three parts. For example, we might set aside 60 percent of the data for training the model, another 20 percent for optimizing the model, and a final 20 percent for testing the model. Apparent performance will drop at each stage. Data from the earliest stages heavily influences the model, while only data from the final stage truly tests the model. The best approach is to loop this process so it trains, optimizes, and tests a model hundreds of times. The distribution of the results of these tests gives a much more accurate picture of how well the model will perform.

Figure 11-1 shows the results of a test we conducted to determine which one of four algorithms best fit a particular sample of data.

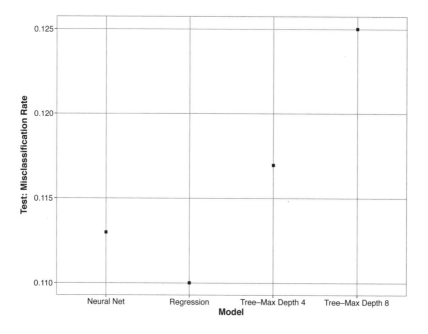

Figure 11-1: Results of a Single Test of Four Algorithms

In this test, the regression model best fit the data (i.e., had the lowest misclassification rate). Had we stopped with this single test, we would have dismissed the other types of models as less accurate. This first test could have been "lucky" or "unlucky." By conducting more tests, we'll get a more accurate measure of our best estimate of true accuracy (the central point in a distribution), as well as its confidence (the spread of the distribution).

After running hundreds of tests using different data sampling, we had a more complete picture. The distribution of results for each modeling algorithm is depicted in the box-and-whisker plot of Figure 11-2.

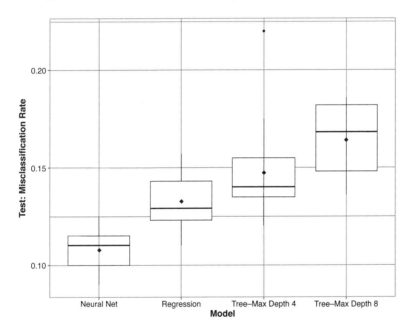

Figure 11-2: Results of Multiple Tests of Four Algorithms

The vertical lines running through the boxes indicate the distribution of the results for each model. Almost all of the data is contained within the bounds of these lines, which are called "whiskers." Outliers are single points outside the bounds of the whiskers. The boxes contain the middle 50 percent of the data (i.e., between the 25th and 75th percentile of the distribution). The diamond inside the box is the mean (average) of the data, and the horizontal line across the middle of the box is the median (middle-valued point).

Note that "Tree-Max Depth 4" has an outlier (with a bad misclassification rate) that draws the mean (diamond) above the *median*. The mean is sensitive to outliers, so the median is a more robust "measure of central tendency." It's also a better metric for comparing modeling techniques when you can only use one number.

After these more extensive tests, it is clear that the neural network outperforms all other models, including the initially promising regression model. This illustrates how a distribution of results gives a much clearer picture of reliability. It also reveals consistency or variance. Note that "Tree-Max Depth 8" has the worst of both, though the outlier associated with "Tree-Max Depth 4" is troubling. A large variance can indicate an unstable model that will give unpredictable and unreliable results. If the variance among the results is small, the mean of the distribution provides a good indication of the performance of the model.

Checking for Mistakes

After reliably measuring out-of-sample (evaluation) performance, the next part of technical validation is ensuring that we avoid making the most common and dangerous model-building mistakes.

Following is a summarized list of what John Elder considers to be the "Top 10 Data Mining Mistakes" in terms of frequency and seriousness.[25] (After compiling the list, John realized that an even more basic problem—mining without proper data—must be addressed as well, so the list actually contains 11 mistakes, numbered 0 through 10.)

THE TOP 10 DATA MINING MISTAKES

Mistake #0: Lacking Labeled Data. A common mistake is to proceed with data analytics projects before sufficient critical data has been gathered. When the probability of interesting events is smaller, the model will need greater amounts of data in order to generalize to unseen cases. To make significant advances with an analysis, you must have labeled cases (i.e., historical cases) for the expected result. For example, an analytics initiative to uncover fraud would need cases that are known to be fraudulent and cases

---

25 Robert Nisbet, John Elder, and Gary Miner (2009) *Handbook of Statistical Analysis and Data Mining Applications*, Academic Press, Chapter 20

that are known to legitimate. In building a model, supervised learning is far preferable to unsupervised learning. (For a refresher on supervised and unsupervised learning, refer to Chapter 2.)

When the necessary data is lacking, sometimes it's possible for an organization to create it. For example, one sophisticated credit-issuing company wanted to consider offering credit to a population of potential customers long thought to be too risky. Since the individuals had never been tested for creditworthiness, the firm didn't have sufficient data to build an accurate credit-scoring model. Therefore, it decided to grant modest amounts of credit almost randomly to thousands of risky applicants and monitor their repayments for two years (at the investment cost of a few million dollars).

With the help of Elder Research, this company built a model that uncovered new patterns and indicators characterizing these potential customers whose applications would normally have been rejected. Programs based on this information allowed our client to safely extend credit to a large portion of this previously underserved population, so that this company's large investment in data analytics resulted in a larger customer base and greater corporate profitability.

Mistake #1: Focusing too much attention on training the model. Using all of the data for training, without reserving any out-of-sample data for evaluation, can result in over-confidence about the model's accuracy. It's as if you're giving the modeling algorithm complete freedom to "take a test while looking at the answers." That's certainly not how we would reliably test students in a classroom, and it shouldn't be the way we test a model!

As previously described in the technical validation section, the best defense against this mistake is to randomly run multiple train/evaluation experiments. This is known as *re-sampling* (examples of specific techniques are bootstrapping, cross-validation, jackknifing, and leave-one-out). Re-sampling simulations answer the question, "How likely is it that a result as good as the model's could have been determined by chance?" An important new version of this concept is discussed in more detail later in this chapter under the heading "Target Shuffling."

Mistake #2: Relying on one technique. You may have heard the saying, "To a little boy with a hammer, all the world's a nail." Unfortunately, many data scientists live this out by trying to use their favorite modeling technique on every problem. Simple regression and decision trees are especially popular with inexperienced modelers, and they may tend to use them almost exclusively. For best results, data scientists should try more than one modeling technique. The biggest expenditure of time and energy is in preparing the data. Once the data has been prepared, one can try five or six different modeling techniques for only about 10 percent additional effort.

Mistake #3: Asking the wrong question. The data scientist should ask the computer to answer questions that are most helpful for the business problem solution, not questions that are easiest to answer. For example, in one of our projects, instead of asking the computer to identify contractors directly who might be at risk of committing fraud, we asked it to identify the contractors who were behaving normally. The client then focused on the outliers as candidates for investigation.

Mistake #4: Listening only to the data. Nothing inside the data itself protects the analyst from achieving a significant but erroneous result. Therefore, the data scientist should always step back and ask if the results produced by the model make sense. For example, John Elder built a model that found a strong state-by-state correlation between lower per-student spending on high school education and higher average SAT scores. Unless you are a fervent foe of government schooling, you will agree that these results run contrary to common sense, because they seem to indicate that spending less money on education increases the quality of education.

Upon further examination, it turned out that the states that spent less on education tended to use ACT test scores as a criterion for entering in-state colleges. In those states, the only students who took the SAT exam were those who planned to go out of state to highly competitive colleges that required it. Not surprisingly, these self-selected top students posted high overall averages on the SAT exam. On the other hand, states that spent more on education typically required all students to take the SAT. Therefore, the students who took the SAT in these states represented a broader range of abilities, which resulted in a lower average of SAT scores for the overall population.

This little story illustrates why it is important to exercise reason, common sense, and domain knowledge when interpreting analytical results. In this example, John needed access to more than the technical method and the data to prevent a completely erroneous conclusion. Domain knowledge enabled him to realize how the different proportions of students in each sample made the comparisons unfair.

Mistake #5: Accepting leaks from the future. This is one of the most common mistakes modelers make, and it's surprising how few realize when they're making it. It occurs when the data scientist builds a model that attempts to use data that wouldn't ordinarily be available until after the model is run. For example, a model that attempts to predict next quarter's

GDP using the current quarter's GDP results might work beautifully on test data, but it wouldn't work in practice, because the government doesn't publish the current quarter's GDP figures until the *end* of the *following* quarter.

In a real-world example, a modeler with a PhD in computer science built a neural network for a Chicago bank to forecast future interest rates. It performed at 95 percent accuracy, which was good . . . actually too good! The bank called in friends of ours to figure out what had gone wrong. When the evaluators looked deeper, they noticed that the model used a version of future interest rates (the output) as one of the inputs. Obviously, it's nonsensical to build a model that relies on data from the future, because that data will not yet be in existence when the model is run. Be very wary of any input that works too well; it's likely a leak from the future.

Mistake #6: Discounting pesky cases. Another common mistake is to discount outliers as data entry errors and unimportant anomalies. In truth, outliers might indicate problems with the flow of information due to a larger business problem, or they might be clues that could open up whole new areas of investigation. For example, the Antarctic Ozone Hole was "discovered" in 1985, yet there were indications of its presence as early as 1981. Scientists initially dismissed the outlying measurements, assuming that the radiation detection sensors were faulty. Odd features in the data, when properly investigated, can lead to some of the best days for data scientists. In fact, we have found that such data discoveries are often as valuable as the full model!

Mistake #7: Extrapolating inappropriately. Data scientists commit this error in a couple of ways. First, they try to extrapolate beyond the limits of the data. For example, they may try to have the model determine automobile gas mileage at eighty miles per hour by extrapolating from a data sample that contains automobile mileage between zero and sixty miles per hour.

Second, they may try to extrapolate based on their own experience. This error arises from the common human tendency to think that we can solve future problems in the same way that we solved similar problems in the past. For example, if our car doesn't start, we may instinctively think that we're out of gas, if that was what caused this problem before. In fact, a frozen fuel line or something else might be causing the problem this time around.

This type of bias, based on experience, can affect model building and interpretation. Inexperienced analysts tend to learn too much from their first few attempts at a new technique. Experienced data scientists and domain experts, on the other hand, avoid making easy assumptions. They have the discipline to separate contributing factors carefully, and they are able to hypothesize a variety of possible explanations for anomalies, which can then be explored and tested.

Mistake #8: Answering every inquiry. This mistake is related to the error of excessive extrapolation (Mistake #7). It occurs when the data scientist asks the model to answer a question that it is not built to answer. Early in his career, John Elder learned (the hard way) to respect the training bounds of the data when he designed a model to estimate the thrust of a rocket engine. One of its inputs was the temperature of the engine, which could be thousands of degrees. The model worked well under normal operating conditions, but one of the client's engineers (who was against the project) insisted that John evaluate the model when the rocket engine was at room temperature. Even though the ridiculous result was expected, it nevertheless created enough doubt about the veracity of the model for management to decide not to use it as intended. It is wise to safeguard against this problem by programming a model to produce the answer "do not know" or "out of bounds" when it is asked to operate outside its normal (training) boundaries.

Skewed data can also produce misleading results. For example, on a model we once built to detect fraud on government contracts, one of the inputs was the number of modifications to the contract. If a contract had two or three modifications, the model gave it the lowest score: one. If it had fifty modifications, the model gave it the highest score: ten. When we ran the model, however, it turned out that a few contracts had 200 or more modifications. This skewed the overall data, so the output of the model didn't make sense. We corrected the problem by programming the model to treat a contract with more than fifty modifications as if it had only fifty. In other words, instead of trying to build the model to answer every inquiry, we modified its features so it did not distinguish between very large numbers, as the exact difference has little meaning beyond a certain limit.

Mistake #9: Careless sampling. Careless sampling can take many forms. One common mistake is "sampling from the top of the file." Here's how it occurs: imagine that you are running a direct-mail campaign and you have a data population that consists of a large number of responses from a broad geographic area. Further imagine that these responses are organized by zip code, and that you want to analyze a portion of them to identify some trends. If you pull your data sample from the top of the file, rather than randomly from throughout the file, you are likely to end up with data samples from relatively few zip codes. A sample from such a limited region may not produce accurate results.

Mistake #10: Only believing the "best" model. Much of what the data scientist learns from the data comes from contrasting how different techniques fit the data in different ways to produce an outcome. Just as it is dangerous to rely on a single technique (Mistake #2), it is also risky to discount a competing model simply because it's not quite as "good" as the best model. Subtle changes in the data may completely shift the performance ranking of models. In fact, the "best" model is likely to be a combination of several good models. One of the simplest ways to create an ensemble of models is to average their outcomes into a single result.[26]

For more information (and more examples) on the most important data mining mistakes and how to avoid them, we refer you to Chapter 20 of *Handbook of Statistical Analysis and Data Mining Applications*[27].

BRYAN'S STORY
Part 8: Validating the Model

As the model came together, the subject-matter experts and testers really started to get excited about the results we were seeing. We put a team of people together to help us determine whether the model's output was valid about actual cases, individual employees, and particular contracts. There was a lot of healthy back and forth with the people who were on the front line of the organization.

Sometimes we learned that what the model said was a problem wasn't really a problem, and we had to modify particular variables we used in the model. We relayed all of this feedback about what was really going on directly to the data scientists, so they could improve the model. As the users began to see what type of results the model could produce, they got more excited about the project and were more willing to help.

---

26 For the most sophisticated and most accurate modeling techniques currently known, see the book by Giovanni Seni and John Elder (2010) *Ensemble Methods in Data Mining: Improving accuracy through combining predictions*, Morgan & Claypool.

27 Robert Nisbet, John Elder, and Gary Miner (2009) *Handbook of Statistical Analysis and Data Mining Applications*, Academic Press.

Checking for Generalization

Once the model is built and optimized, using training data, we want to know how well it will "generalize" from this training to make accurate predictions on data it will see for the first time. This validation process uses a "holdout sample" of the original data that we reserved in the beginning for this purpose. The model has never seen this data before this step because we held it out for this purpose and did not use it to build and test the model.

Ideally, the model should fit the training data well, but not exactly. A model that fits its training data too well will not generalize well (assuming there is "noise" in the data, which there always is). When confronted with new, unseen data, such a model will produce results that have less accuracy and a higher variance. This "over-fit" is less likely to occur when we validate a model using a distribution of results instead of a single result.

Using Experts to Qualify Model Results

Once a fitted model has begun to produce reliable analytic results, as measured purely from a data science perspective, SMEs are again needed to qualify the results from a business perspective. Computers, even IBM's Watson, are just machines. They still lack the ability of the human brain to connect the context and semantics of information. Successful data analytics projects employ the complementary strengths of humans and computers.

The advantage of human involvement can be illustrated on an elementary level by the famous Anscombe's quartet. The table in Figure 11-3 shows a set of data in which there are four (x,y) pairs of interest: XY_1, XY_2, XY_3, and X_4Y_4. Interestingly, the measures of fit, error, and correlation for these four sets of data are exactly the same:

All have the same measure of correlation: $\rho_{xy} = 0.85$

All have the same regression line, which minimizes squared error:

   yLS = 3 + 0.5x

All have the same mean squared error: MSE = 1.25

All have the same degree of variance reduction: $R^2 = 0.67$

X	Y₁	Y₂	Y₃	X₄	Y₄
10	8.04	9.14	7.46	8	6.58
8	6.95	8.14	6.77	8	5.76
13	7.58	8.74	12.74	8	7.71
9	8.81	8.77	7.11	8	8.84
11	8.33	9.26	7.81	8	8.47
14	9.96	8.10	8.84	8	7.04
6	7.24	6.13	6.08	8	5.25
4	4.26	3.10	5.39	19	12.50
12	10.84	9.13	8.15	8	5.56
7	4.82	7.26	6.42	8	7.91
5	5.68	4.74	5.73	8	6.89

$$\rho_{xy} = 0.85$$

$$y_{LS} = 3 + 0.5x$$

$$MSE = 1.25$$

$$R^2 = 0.67$$

Figure 11-3: Four Model Metrics of Four Pairs of Variables

The computer "sees" the data through these kinds of summary statistics. To the computer, all four pairs look the same. Yet, if we plot the data, the human eye can instantly recognize major differences, as shown in Figure 11-4. The upper-left plot is probably what we expected—a positive trend line with noise. The upper-right plot is a parabola, which would be exactly fit by a quadratic model (one with an x^2 term). The lower-left plot has an output outlier that pulls the fitting line strongly toward it. (All of the other ten points are on a different straight line). Finally, the bottom-left plot has a *leverage* point—an input outlier—which defines the whole slope of the line (hence the term "leverage").

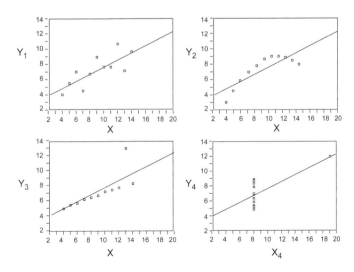

Figure 11-4: Plots of the Four Data Sets

Anscombe cleverly designed the datasets to fool the computer, but in these low dimensions, humans can clearly distinguish these important properties. In higher dimensions, we'd need a clue indicating where to look. So, when building and validating analytical models, use the computer to find what it can, but also employ human judgment and common sense to explore possibilities and test the results.

Target Shuffling

Recently, many studies have shown that 65-95 percent of epidemiology findings in medical and pharmaceutical journal articles (to use a dramatic example) cannot be replicated[28]. This shocking result means that the majority of the data relationships that medical researchers identify as correlations are actually spurious. Have you ever wondered why some studies have reported that coffee is good for you, and other studies have reported just the opposite? Now you know!

There are two primary reasons for this problem. First, the business of medical research primarily rewards findings that are (at least apparently) positive ("A leads to B"), and not ones that are merely confirmatory ("Yes, just as they said.") or negative ("Nothing found here."). Likewise, medical journals tend to report on an experiment that leads to correlations, real or spurious, and ignore dozens of other studies that show no result. Second, researchers are using the wrong metric of significance, which can make a finding seem ten times or even one hundred times more significant than it really is.

Focusing on the second reason mentioned above, note that an increase in data volume, especially in input variables (x), increases the probability of statistically interesting results. The larger the number of candidate input variables, the better the chance that one will line up well with the output. Therefore, as the data scientist gets more and more data, the likelihood increases that a model will misidentify some random associations as meaningful correlations. This is what Elder Research calls the *vast search effect*.

In these larger data sets, sufficient time must be spent validating and evaluating the results to ensure that they are revealing actual phenomena, rather than simply random incidents. One way to evaluate these interesting correlations is through "target shuffling," a technique that John Elder intro-

---

28 For interesting and somewhat controversial reading on this issue, see "Trouble at the Lab; Unreliable Research." *Economist* (US) 19 Oct. 2013; and, "How Science Goes Wrong." *Economist (US)* 19 Oct. 2013.

duced to the modern analytical world. We say "modern" analytical world, because after he "invented" it, he discovered that the basic idea had actually been conceived generations before. But, since it requires the processing power of computers to work effectively, it had never gained popularity.

Target shuffling provides a measure of how likely it is that you could have achieved as good a result just by chance. If the shuffled data provides a result that's as good as the actual model's result, we know that the actual model's result is not that good. Stated statistically, since true statistical significance is the extent to which a result is better than that expected to arise simply from random variation or errors in sampling, we know that the actual model's result is not significant.

Target shuffling[29] uses simulation to repeat the search for results extensively. The "shuffling" is achieved by randomly reassigning the output value (target outcome) of each observation (i.e., each row in the data) to a different observation. (To refresh your memory about target outcomes and observations, see Figure 2-3 in Chapter 2.) The data scientist applies the modeling process[30] to this shuffled dataset and measures the interestingness (such as apparent significance) of the best finding (i.e., the best performance of the model).

The unique part is that all the shuffled datasets are designed to simulate randomness. In each experiment, only the target vectors (the historical values of the thing we are trying to predict) are shuffled. The input vectors (predictors) are left untouched, and the existing relationships between the predictors still hold.

By repeating this process many times, the scientist is able to create a distribution of the "performances" that can be extracted from data known to be random. We can ascertain the true statistical significance of the original model by comparing the results derived from the real, original data to the results contained in this distribution of "best apparent discoveries" (BADs).

For instance, if 150 of 1,000 BADs are better than the true model, the true model has a 15 percent significance value. Remember that we are trying to determine whether our model results are real or simply obtained by random chance (i.e., whether our prediction is better than "rolling the dice"). By comparing our model results with the results obtained when we

---

29 Shuffling denotes random reordering or sampling without replacement.

30 Applying a modeling process would entail re-training the model on the shuffled data.

purposefully create random chance in the data, we get a more accurate understanding of model performance.

Just as it's a good idea to try multiple modeling methods to see which model works best on the data, it's advantageous to try multiple techniques to validate a model. Target shuffling is a powerful validation technique that offers at least the following three advantages over other validation techniques.

1. Because of the tremendous computing power available today, it is possible, and fairly simple, to use target shuffling to simulate results that are more accurate than single measures of statistical significance.

2. Target shuffling is more intuitively understandable than other techniques and, consequently, non-statisticians will more readily believe its results.

3. The target shuffling technique is highly useful for confirming and double-checking a result that has been calculated statistically.

All of these reasons make target shuffling well worth incorporating into your organization's analytic practices. To gain a better understanding of the vast search effect, target shuffling, and some of the subtleties of data mining, we refer you to the tutorial paper in the Appendix, written by our colleagues Ben Bullard and John Elder, "Are Orange Cars Really Least Likely to be Lemons?"

Business Validation

Business validation is less concerned with how well the model fits the data than with how well the model meets its business objectives. For instance, if you're the Inspector General of a government agency and you want to identify vendors who are potentially committing fraud, one of your goals is to minimize false positives so your investigators don't waste time auditing honest vendors. Therefore, in order to more economically utilize your investigators and maximize the overall productivity of your department, you might adjust how you use your model to maximize return for available effort, even though this will allow a few miscreants to escape. That is, it will allow some false negatives.

Accomplishing this does not require modifications to the model itself. You simply need to adjust where the model draws the line on its predictions between what is fraudulent and what is not. Testing the model on data that contains known cases of fraud will tell you how well the model fits this business purpose.

On the other hand, if the purpose of the model is early detection of cancer, you might want to tune the model so that it puts more emphasis on minimizing false negatives. In other words, since cancer is best treated when detected early, you may be willing to tolerate a certain percentage of false positives in order to minimize missed positives. Even though false positives are alarming for a time, they can be confirmed or dismissed by additional testing. From an overall perspective, even the cost of unnecessary treatment may be a good investment if it helps avoid missing true cases. The optimal trade-offs between types of mistakes depend on the nature of the problem being solved.

This adjustment of error trade-off has nothing to do with how the model is built. It simply relates to where the model draws the line between what is considered cancerous and what is not. There is always a trade-off between these two types of mistakes; the users of the models and the business domain experts are in the best position to provide guidance about the relative importance of minimizing false dismissals vs. false alarms. To just minimize the number of errors falsely assumes that all mistakes are equally bad.

It's easy to understand why many data miners attempt shortcuts around the validation stage of the model-building process. For most of them, building the model is the fun part. Validating a model can be laborious, and it's no fun when the results turn out to be less than satisfactory, but skimping on this step can lead to expensive mistakes.

No model can be considered complete without validation. If you're the manager of a data mining project, make sure the model builder runs several validation tests, not just one. Keep testing until you are confident that the model works as planned.

Chapter Nuggets

- Shortcuts in validation will cause serious problems later. Data scientists and domain experts should always step back and ask if the results produced by the model make sense.
- Technical validation checks how well the model performs on new data.
- Business validation checks how well the model satisfies its business purpose.
- Elder's "The Top 10 Data Mining Mistakes" is a useful checklist for ensuring that analysts avoid the errors most likely to impair a model's utility.

- Once a fitted model produces reliable out-of-sample results, subject-matter experts (SMEs) are again needed to qualify the results from a business perspective.
- Target shuffling is a powerful technique to determine how likely it is that you could have achieved as good a result just by chance, which is the true definition of statistical significance.

CHAPTER 12

DEPLOYING THE MODEL

After constructing and validating the model, the next (and final) step is deployment. Building a model in a controlled environment can be a challenge, but making that model work in an actual business environment is even more difficult. Typically, this phase involves much more than simply installing a completed model. It can entail a significant amount of development work on the model and require extensive changes to complex, repeatable business processes throughout the organization. In a large enterprise, hundreds or even thousands of people may need to be retrained. In fact, deployment is sometimes more expensive and time-consuming than all other phases combined.

Surprisingly, many organizations neglect to plan and budget for deployment. After carefully considering what kind of model they need, who's going to build it, how they're going to pay for it, and what kind of ROI they can expect, they fail to plan how they're going to put it into use. Even the best analytics output is valueless until it is integrated into existing organizational processes and accepted within the organization's culture. It's exciting to build an impressive model and discover useful insights, but a positive ROI depends on effective implementation.

Model deployment should be an integral part of the initial planning for more reasons than just budget and schedule. For one thing, the model's impact on institutional processes can influence the choice of modeling technique. In an environment where everyone is familiar with operating by rule-based systems, a neural network would be difficult or impossible to implement, while a decision tree model might be easy to introduce.

Planning and Budgeting for Deployment

In the deployment phase, a handoff of responsibilities typically occurs. The analytics team moves into more of an advisory role, and the information technology (IT) or business application people come to the fore. Analytical skills become less important. Familiarity with the operations of the business and skills in computer engineering, computer architecture, data governance, information technology, and networking become more important.

Some clients mistakenly assume that the completion of the model means the completion of the project, but the project is not successful until the model is successfully deployed. That's why we repeatedly emphasize to our clients the importance of planning and budgeting for the deployment phase. It's difficult for us to detail to our clients how to budget for deployment, however, because the costs will depend to a significant degree on the nature of the client's business and the capabilities and dedication of the client's staff.

Business Processes Are Key

When planning for deployment, start by identifying which business processes will use the results of the model. From that, determine the end users, the applications that might be affected, and the maintenance that will be required.

The following questions will facilitate this planning process.

1. End-user consumption:
   - Who is going to use the model output?
   - What tools are they familiar with?
   - Are the end users technical or non-technical?
   - What type of work do they do on a day-to-day basis?

2. Business process:
   - Which business process or processes are impacted?
   - Is the process currently supported by a software application?
   - Who is responsible for updates/changes to the software application?
   - How many users will need access to the model results?

3. Maintenance and refresh:
   - How will we know 12, 18, and 24 months from now if the model is still valid?
   - Who is going to upgrade or fix the model when it degrades or breaks?
   - How often does the data need to be refreshed?
   - How are we going to get access to regular updates of the data?

Example: Finding Taxpayer Fraud

A case study about taxpayer fraud will illustrate how complex this deployment phase can be. Let's assume the tax-collecting agency wants to implement a new analytics model to detect potential cases of fraud on individual and business tax returns.

The first requirement in the deployment phase will be to figure out how to feed the model all of the relevant data from the millions of returns filed each year. This is more challenging than it might initially seem. The body of each return has very many pieces of information, and even a simple return can have several different supporting schedules. In addition, complex regulations usually govern how the agency must process these returns, and elected officials often may change these rules on short notice. What's more, this entire operation must satisfy very serious security restrictions and real-time operational requirements.

Even after determining how to capture all of this data on a real-time basis, we still have to address the big issue of deciding what to do with the information. Suppose the purpose of the model is to flag tax returns that indicate some degree of risk of fraud. What kind of actions should this flag trigger? Should the system generate a letter to the taxpayer based on that particular risk? Should the model refer the case to the audit department, or perhaps to law enforcement? How should these departments handle this information within their workflow? The answers to these questions will dictate the extent of the changes to the organization's systems and procedures.

Admittedly, this is an extreme example. On the other end of the spectrum, we might have a financial model that is used for budgeting only once a year. A financial analyst with experience in the model-building process might be able to run this model each year simply by feeding it the most recent year's data.

However, even some simplistic analytics models can require considerable thought about systematizing input data and presenting output results. For example, internal organizational systems may need to be monitored and occasionally changed to ensure that the data fed to a financial budgeting model each year is accurate and consistent.

In fact, the deployment phase can require such agility, that we believe the CRISP-DM process, which was designed more for discovery than implementation, is not the best framework for handling it. Instead, we recommend some of the processes used today for software and networking system development.

BRYAN'S STORY
Part 9: Deploying the Model

Some of the first models we built were really good, but we presented the output in a spreadsheet format, and very few investigators took the time to understand what the output meant. So, we made the model more user friendly by having it anticipate the next questions investigators were going to ask. For example, when the model presented certain data about possible travel expense fraud, experienced investigators told us that they next would want to see the details of the employee's travels. So, we put a link in the program that would bring up the travel vouchers. That made the model a one-stop source of information. Investigators no longer had to dig for the data they needed; it jumped out at them in a very intuitive way.

With these links, investigators could research cases on the fly. For instance, the data might flag a particular healthcare case as suspicious because of the age of the employee, the type of doctor the person was seeing, and the amount of money involved. So, the investigator might decide to look at more invoices for this doctor or more cases for this employee. The model would give the investigator enough information to understand exactly what was going on.

Four Important Questions

When we discussed the process for understanding the business in Chapter 8, we mentioned that our data scientists strive to consult with representatives of everyone in the organization who affects the inputs of the model or is impacted by its output. These conversations require considerable time, and often our clients wonder why we need to talk to so many people.

The answer should now be clear. In order to ensure that the model will function as desired, we must fully understand how it fits into the organizational environment. A good model is designed with the ends in mind. Involving people in the preliminary phases promotes operational success and user buy-in.

When planning the deployment phase, we seek to answer 4 questions.

1. **What business processes will consume the results of the model?** In other words, who will use the output of the model to modify what they do? What business processes will need to change on a day-to-day basis to take advantage of the model's results? For example, a company that wants to increase the sales effectiveness of its customer service representatives might build

a model to display product recommendations tailored to the customer who is on the phone. Assembling this type of information would take hours or even weeks for an individual because it would require examining the past buying behaviors of each customer in light of the company's current product offerings. However, a model properly integrated with the company's business systems could produce this information instantly.

2. **How quickly and frequently should the model generate results?** The answer depends on the use of the model. For example, Google must generate its search engine results in real time to be effective. Likewise, a model to detect credit card fraud must instantly monitor all credit card transactions and score each one. On the other hand, a model that detects potential fraud on government contracts may need to produce results only monthly, and a financial planning model may need to produce reports only annually.

3. **How will the data be made available?** Ensuring that data is available for model operation on a consistent basis can be a challenging task. For example, a financial model might need information from several different systems about invoices cut, checks written, cash received, refunds given, contracts entered into, contracts modified, and so on. It may not be terribly difficult for an individual or individuals to provide samples of this data for purposes of building the model, but it will require a much greater level of sophistication and effort to automatically gather this data from the various systems and deliver it to the model on an on-going basis.

4. **How will the company monitor and maintain the model?** Microeconomic changes within the organization and macroeconomic events in the marketplace can dramatically affect the performance of a model. Within a company, for example, data fields on input documents can change, often without notice. In the overall economy, changes in economic conditions can affect consumer behaviors, which in turn can affect a model's accuracy.

All models should be periodically back-tested with current data, either automatically or manually, to ensure that they continue to make relevant predictions. Back-testing is especially important for applications like stock trading, consumer purchasing habits, and political advertising, which can be significantly impacted by changing economic conditions, political developments, and fads. Just as you wouldn't drive a car without periodically servicing it, you shouldn't operate a model without periodically back-testing and maintaining it.

Chapter Nuggets

- Building a model in a controlled environment is a challenge, but making that model work in an actual business environment can be an even bigger challenge.
- Model deployment should be an integral part of the initial planning, not only because it can require budgeting considerable money and personnel, but also because the model's impact on institutional processes can influence the choice of modeling methods.
- When planning the deployment phase, we seek to answer four questions:
  1. What business processes will consume the results of the model?
  2. How quickly and frequently should the model generate results?
  3. How will the data be made available?
  4. How will the company monitor and maintain the model?
- All models should be periodically back-tested with current data to ensure that they continue to make relevant predictions.

CHAPTER 13

REALIZING THE TRANSFORMATION

In this primer we have given you an overview of how to use data mining and predictive analytics to increase your organization's success. You now have the basic information you need to competently participate in and lead data analytics initiatives.

This knowledge, although essential, is not sufficient to ensure that your analytics projects meet your goals. Your best efforts will fall short unless your organization has a culture that fosters innovation. If the culture does not value creativity, encourage experimentation, and tolerate the risk of failure, it will resist the revolutionary changes that analytics projects can precipitate.

Organizations that effectively use data analytics undergo a transformation in the way they think. Instead of *reactively* focusing on past events, management begins to *proactively* focus on potential. Instead of making decisions based almost exclusively on reports about what *has* happened, the organization begins to rely on predictions about what is *likely* to happen and why.

Realizing the Potential

Analytics projects require focused, steady attention in order to realize their full potential. One reason is because the computer models themselves tend to degrade over time. This happens not because the software deteriorates, but because the environments in which the models operate are in constant flux. Changes in available data, economic conditions, organizational policies and procedures, laws and regulations, and technology can all impact the performance of a model.

A second reason is because the analytic process depends on people. Once an organization has experienced some degree of analytics success, the novelty may start to wear off. Management may think the organization can coast, while continuing to enjoy the full benefits of an initiative. Some people involved in the process may begin to lose focus and reorder their priorities.

Referring again to the gardening analogy, analytics projects must be diligently tended in order to bear fruit. Old habits die hard, and without steady instruction and encouragement, the organization may revert to old ways of making decisions.

The Tipping Point

In the early stages of an analytics initiative, it's natural for some people or groups within the organization to feel threatened. In particular, information technology (IT) people and those who monitor the efficiency and productivity of marketing, finances, or other functions of the organization may worry that analytics will diminish the importance of their jobs and the funding for their departments.

In our experience, that is very rarely the case. We find that a successful analytics initiative will usually focus more attention on the importance of analysis. It will empower analysts, IT professionals, and others who deal with data to be more productive. And management usually reinvests the savings, so that the very areas that felt threatened may actually experience an increase in funding.

In analytics, perseverance is crucial. Organizations must maintain momentum and stay the course in order to realize the benefits. Those that do persevere will eventually experience a tipping point, as users of the data-driven results will begin to rely on this output and ask for more. Management will begin to find more problems that analytics can solve, and they will devote more resources to the task.

BRYAN'S STORY
Part 10: Realizing the Transformation

After we started using the new models, investigators began solving more cases in fewer hours. They also became more proactive, which was a huge shift from the reactive approach of most law enforcement organizations. They began to ask, "Why are we working the $100,000 cases, when we could be working $1 million cases?" As investigators began to return more and more dollars to the Postal Service, they got hungrier and hungrier for data. They began to proactively drill into the data and ask for more. I can remember the first time an investigator called and said, "Hey, when are you going to refresh this data?" That's when we knew that we were over the hump with data analytics.

One of our investigators said in a conference presentation to a bunch of other investigators, "I didn't believe in analytics. I didn't understand it. I thought it was another gimmick, but now that I have used it, it's made my life a whole lot easier. I'm able to work more cases and bigger cases, and I close them faster."

When investigators started telling other investigators that data mining was the real deal, analytics usage surged, and a tipping point occurred. We no longer had to beg them to use the model, and we no longer had to beg management to give us resources. In fact, we began having trouble managing all the work that was coming our way.

This early win with workers' compensation allowed us to explain the value of analytics in terms people could understand, and it paved the way for programs in mail theft, financial fraud, and contract fraud. Our portfolio grew to the point where it began to drive strategic change in the organization at the macro level.

For instance, it changed the way we assigned investigators to areas. In the past, the head of investigations might have allocated our investigators evenly among the Postal Service's four program areas, simply because that was the way it had always been done. Analytics, however, provided a picture of the battlefield landscape. Instead of deploying the same number of investigators to each area, management could position them according to where theft was occurring or was likely to occur. They started saying things like, "Let's shift some resources from financial to health-care fraud, and let's shift resources from Wisconsin to Miami." The organization became more nimble. In the past, it would have been too risky to make changes on the fly because we didn't have the information on which to base those decisions.

Today, data analytics is an integral part of our organization. It has evolved from start-up status to a production-based program that is seen as a vital component of our long-term plan for increasing productivity.

Bryan Jones, formerly with the U.S. Postal Service Office of Inspector General, is just one of the many executives we know who have discovered the power of data mining and predictive analytics. Now that you know something about how these tools work and what they can do, we hope you will discover for yourself that data analytics is the "real deal!"

Chapter Nuggets

- Your efforts will best succeed when your organization has a culture that fosters innovation, values creativity, encourages experimentation, and tolerates the risk of failure. Rigid, risk-averse organizations resist the revolutionary changes that analytics projects can precipitate.
- Organizations that effectively use data analytics undergo a transformation in the way they think. Instead of reactively focusing on past events, management begins to proactively focus on potential. Instead of making decisions based largely on what has happened, the organization begins to rely on predictions about what is likely to happen, and why.
- In analytics, perseverance is crucial. Organizations must stay the course in order to realize the benefits. Those that persevere will eventually experience a tipping point, where the positive benefits of the effort begin to persuade others to trust and rely on the process.

APPENDIX

Are Orange Cars Really Least Likely to be Lemons?

by
Ben Bullard & John Elder
Elder Research, Inc.

A recent article in *The Seattle Times* reported ". . . an orange used car is least likely to be a lemon." This discovery surfaced in a competition hosted by Kaggle to predict bad buys among used cars using historical data. Of the 72,983 used cars, 8,976 were labeled bad buys (12.3%). Yet, of the 415 orange cars in the dataset, only 34 were bad (8.2%). The full breakdown of bad-buy proportion by car color is shown in Table 1 and Figure 1 below, where the low proportion of bad buys among orange cars stands out prominently.

Table 1: Bad Buys by Color

Row	Color	Count	Bad Buys	Percent
1	SILVER	14875	1843	12.39%
2	WHITE	12123	1506	12.42%
3	BLUE	10347	1189	11.49%
4	GREY	7887	911	11.55%
5	BLACK	7627	858	11.25%
6	RED	6257	825	13.19%
7	GOLD	5231	737	14.09%
8	GREEN	3194	402	12.59%
9	MAROON	2046	260	12.71%
10	BEIGE	1584	211	13.32%
11	BROWN	436	56	12.84%
12	ORANGE	415	34	8.19%
13	PURPLE	373	56	15.01%
14	YELLOW	244	34	13.93%
15	OTHER	242	29	11.98%
16	NOT AVAIL	94	24	25.53%
17	NULL	8	1	12.50%
18	TOTAL	72983	8976	12.30%

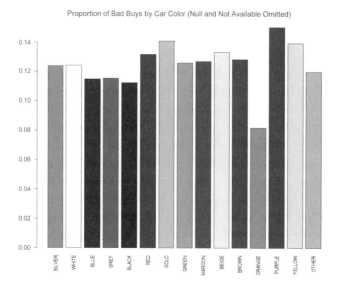

Figure 1

How unusual is this low proportion? In other words, assuming the true proportion is actually equal, what is the likelihood that it could have occurred by chance for a random partition of that size? Such a calculation takes into account the numbers of cars making up both proportions (good and bad orange vs. good and bad non-orange[31].) A 1-sided statistical hypothesis test for equality of proportions between two samples yields a p-value of 0.00675 (see Equation 1). In other words, the hypothesis test reveals that if the underlying reality is that the proportion of bad buys among orange cars is really the same as among all other cars, then the probability that one would observe a sample proportion for orange cars that is so much lower than the sample proportion for non-orange cars (given sample sizes of 415 and 72,466, respectively) is only 0.675%.

> prop.test(c(34,8917), c(415,72466), alternative="less")$p.value (Eqn. 1 in R code)

[1] 0.006754577

Given such a low p-value, it seems likely that orange cars really are better buys. Put another way, since the default or "null" hypothesis (that the

---

31 Note that NULL and NOT AVAIL were removed from the analysis altogether throughout this paper. This was due to small sample size as well as the lack of explanation as to why the color of the car was not reported.

proportions are actually equal) is less than 1% likely, there's more than a 99% chance that the alternative hypothesis (that orange cars are really good buys) is true.

Interpretation

Why orange? With such a finding it is almost inevitable that we will cast about for an explanation. The *Seattle Times* reports, "As for why orange used cars are most likely to be in good shape, the numbers did not hold the answer. One notion was that flashy colors attract car fanatics who would be more likely to take care of their vehicles. That didn't pan out, however, since the least well-kept cars turned out to be purple."

Brainstorming, we wondered if, perhaps, orange cars are made by only a few manufacturers, or if they only represent a few makes or models, or years of production. If that's the case, perhaps orange is confounded (mixed up with) another variable actually related to reliability. In other words, the color orange might not be a cause, but a "tag-along" effect. A colleague suggested that orange may be more visible to other drivers, and thus those cares are involved in fewer collisions. The opportunity for speculation is endless!

Two comments here:
1. To examine these questions in depth would involve building a data mining model from the full set of Kaggle contest data, which included many other variables.
2. We have learned to distrust the interpretability of a model. It's easy (and dangerous) to invent explanations of why some finding might be true *after* a finding is made!

At this point, we decided to move from testing the hypothesis that first leapt out to explore what the true findings should be. What colors are most interesting in relation to reliability, and how confident are we in those results?

This paper establishes a framework for approaching problems of this kind. It shows how the immediate finding might not be the most interesting. Secondly, it demonstrates how the likelihood of finding something only by chance that appears interesting is much greater than traditional statistical tests reveal. And lastly, it explains Target Shuffling[32] as an accurate way to answer that key statistical question: How likely could a result as strong as this have occurred by chance?

Where Did Our Hypothesis Come From?

As we consider the strength of our conclusion about orange cars, the first thing we should note is that the hypothesis was only developed after seeing the data. No one surmised it and then went out and collected data to test that idea. Rather, data was collected and the graph revealed that orange is an outlier. Then we applied a hypothesis test to its numbers.

The importance of this distinction is probably not obvious, but it can be made clearer by a simple illustration. Imagine that I report to you the results of a test I ran to determine if a coin is fair. I flipped the coin 10 times and discovered that it landed heads every single time. Applying a hypothesis test, I find that I can reject the null hypothesis (that the coin is fair) with a p-value of 0.00195[33]. In other words, there is only a 0.195% chance that a fair coin would land heads on all 10 flips. So we could conclude (at a 99.8% confidence level) that this coin must not be fair. It is actually still possible for the coin to be fair, but the hypothesis test tells us how unlikely that is.

If I reported to you that I next tested another 999 coins and found that all 1,000 of them landed heads every single time, you would likely be convinced beyond all doubt that there is something fishy about the whole lot of them. We can't imagine flipping 10,000 coins and getting 10,000 heads and 0 tails. All of the coins must surely be biased!

However, if I then mentioned in passing that I had also happened to test 999,000 other coins, which resulted in a variety of other proportions of heads and tails, would that change things? These are all separate coins, and I have not repeated trials of any of the earlier coins I told you about. Every test is independent; they don't affect each other. So, what difference does it make that these other 999,000 coins behaved more randomly? They don't even relate to the first 1,000 coins.

Intuitively, though, you know the two groups of coins cannot be considered completely independent. You would want to know right away whether

---

32 Target Shuffling has been employed by one of us—intermittently, but to great effect—for 20 years, but was first written up in 2009 in Chapter 13 of the *Handbook of Statistical Analysis & Data Mining Applications*, by Nisbet, Elder, and Miner.

33 Probability of 10 consecutive heads or tails with a fair coin is 0.5^10 or 1/1024. Therefore the *p*-value for a 2-sided test would be 2/1024 or 0.00195.

I identified the 1,000 coins that always landed heads ahead of time, or if I first tested all 1,000,000 together and only picked out the 1,000 afterward. You know that if I were to test 1,000,000 coins, I would expect some of them to land heads every single time, even if every single one was fair. In fact, if you do the math[34], you will find that one would expect 977 out of 1,000,000 coins to land heads all ten times on average. Therefore, finding 1,000 coins that landed all heads is not surprising at all, and it should not be used as evidence to suggest that those 1,000 coins are biased[35]. The expected distribution of each outcome (i.e., 9 of 10) is shown in Figure 2 and Table 2.

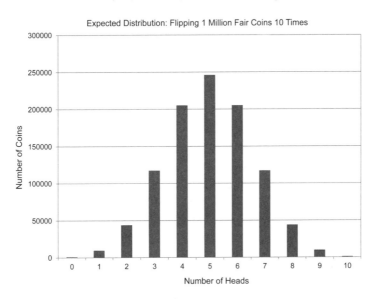

Figure 2

Table 2

Heads	Percent	Count
0	0.1%	977
1	1.0%	9,766
2	4.4%	43,945
3	11.7%	117,188
4	20.5%	205,078

34 1,000,000 * 0.5^10 = 976.56

35 One could *hypothesize*, however, based on this finding, that these 1,000 coins are biased and run a subsequent test on these particular coins to gain evidence either supporting or refuting this hypothesis.

5	24.6%	246,094
6	20.5%	205,078
7	11.7%	117,188
8	4.4%	43,945
9	1.0%	9,766
10	0.1%	977

This simple example shows that the significance of the finding that 1,000 coins landed all heads depends entirely on whether or not I had hypothesized *ahead of time* that these particular coins were biased, and the other 999,000 not, or if I simply tested all 1,000,000 coins indiscriminately and picked out the 1,000 based on the results.

In the same way, for our present investigation involving orange cars, it's important to point out that we arrived at the hypothesis that orange cars are good buys only *after* viewing the data. Had the data been different, the hypothesis itself would have changed. Obviously, if green cars, for instance, had happened to have a strikingly low proportion of bad buys, we would have tested the hypothesis that green cars are good buys.

If we assume that the true proportion of bad buys among all cars for all colors is actually identical, the probability that one would find a statistically significant difference between red cars and non-red cars is low, and the probability that one would find a statistically significant difference between green cars and non-green cars is low. However, the probability that one would find a statistically significant difference between *some* color car and all other colored cars might not be that low! In fact, if the number of colors was great enough, the prospect of finding a statistically significant difference would be almost certain (just as in the case of finding a thousand coins that land heads 10 times in a row if we flip 1 million of them).

What we see is that statistical hypothesis tests only work when the hypothesis comes first and the analysis second. One cannot use the data to create the hypothesis and then use traditional statistical tests to score that hypothesis on the same data. That leads to "overfit" and over-confidence in your results, which leads to the model underperforming (or failing entirely) on new data, where it is most needed.

The Danger of Vast Search

How do we know what to hypothesize? Isn't the great strength of data mining that the computer can try out all sorts of things and report back which ones work?

Yes, we can and should use data to develop our hypotheses, but we must then test those hypotheses on unseen data. To get an idea of the significance of a finding without such unseen data, we have to ask a broader question than how likely is this exact finding to have occurred by chance. We have to ask, "How likely is it that *any* finding *this interesting* could occur by chance?"

Data mining is subject to the power and peril of what we call the "vast search effect." If we search hard enough over enough variables, we are sure to find *something* "interesting," whether that finding is real or the effect of random chance. Hypothesis tests are supposed to tell us how likely it is that our finding could have happened by chance, but they fail to do so accurately when the hypothesis itself is contingent on the very same data against which it is tested.

Does this mean that orange cars aren't exceptionally good buys after all? No, they still could be. However, this does mean that the *p*-value we originally calculated is misleading. We must either take into account the fact that we both developed and tested our hypothesis using the same data, or we must find new data on which to test our hypothesis in order to calculate a more accurate probability. Three possible approaches to doing this are described below.

Solution 1: Partitioning

As mentioned previously, there is nothing wrong with using data to develop hypotheses. A glance at Figure 1 reveals that the proportion of bad buys among orange cars is lower than that of other colors. Unexpected, data-driven hypotheses like this often lead to novel and beneficial discoveries. To really test this hypothesis, we should now go out, collect data on a new group of used cars, and see how well it holds up.

However, this is easier said than done! It takes a lot of work to survey thousands of used car buyers to see if the car panned out or not (and over what time frame, etc.). Instead, we can partition the data to mimic repeated experiments. The idea is very simple. After receiving the dataset (in this case 72,983 records) and *before* analyzing it, the data scientist splits it into a training partition and a testing (or evaluation) partition. If the cases are not independent, this split must be done carefully, perhaps, for example, according to time. Here, however, it may be done randomly.

The goal is to make the testing data simulate *future* data. Often one uses, say, 70% of the data for training and the remaining 30% for testing. The analyst employs the training dataset to build a model or explore the data to come up with a hypothesis. Then he or she employs the testing dataset to test that model or hypothesis on unseen data. The test step simulates the use of the model in the real world.

There are a few things to watch out for when testing the data. For example, if this test is performed too often (i.e., if there are too many iterations of training), the test data can become partly "known" to the user/model, and it will lose some of its power to simulate future reality. Also, the test data might—randomly sampled or not—be too different from the training data for a single sample to be used as the quality measure. We therefore recommend cross-validation, or bootstrapping, to improve the quality of testing.

Unfortunately, it is theoretically too late to reserve data, now that we've explored it. Nevertheless, it is still worth doing, and we'll demonstrate how.

Imagine that we have just received the 72,983 cases of used cars labeled with color and quality. Ideally, we might partition it according to time. But because we do not have that information, we will randomly partition the dataset into 60% training and 40% testing (Table 3). Afterwards, our training proportion looks like Figure 3 and Table 3.

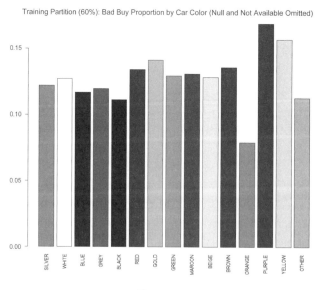

Training Partition (60%): Bad Buy Proportion by Car Color (Null and Not Available Omitted)

Figure 3

Table 3

Row	Color	Count	Bad Buys	Percent
1	SILVER	8,858	1,080	12.19%
2	WHITE	7,233	919	12.71%
3	BLUE	6,210	726	11.69%
4	GREY	4,709	563	11.96%
5	BLACK	4,593	511	11.13%
6	RED	3,749	503	13.42%
7	GOLD	3,136	443	14.13%
8	GREEN	1,893	245	12.94%
9	MAROON	1,223	160	13.08%
10	BEIGE	935	120	12.83%
11	BROWN	280	38	13.57%
12	ORANGE	253	20	7.91%
13	PURPLE	231	39	16.88%
14	YELLOW	153	24	15.69%
15	OTHER	142	16	11.27%
18	TOTAL	43,598	5,407	12.40%

Based on this training dataset (and pretending we have never seen the full dataset!), we would still hypothesize that the orange car proportion is interestingly low. It is conceivable that we could have chosen a partition that would not have readily led to this hypothesis, but in this case orange remains an obvious outlier. Now, let's assume that we wish to test the hypothesis that orange cars have a lower proportion of bad buys than non-orange cars. Our testing dataset (Table 4) looks like Figure 4.

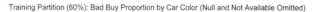

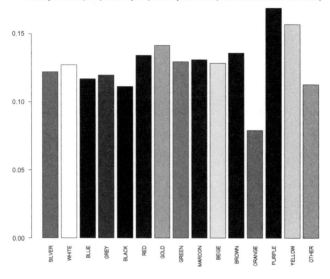

Training Partition (60%): Bad Buy Proportion by Car Color (Null and Not Available Omitted)

Figure 4

Table 4: Test Dataset (Remaining 40% sample)

Row	Color	Count	Bad Buys	Percent
1	SILVER	6,017	763	12.68%
2	WHITE	4,890	587	12.00%
3	BLUE	4,137	463	11.19%
4	GREY	3,178	348	10.95%
5	BLACK	3,034	347	11.44%
6	RED	2,508	322	12.84%
7	GOLD	2,095	294	14.03%
8	GREEN	1,301	157	12.07%
9	MAROON	823	100	12.15%
10	BEIGE	649	91	14.02%
11	BROWN	156	18	11.54%
12	ORANGE	162	14	8.64%
13	PURPLE	142	17	11.97%
14	YELLOW	91	10	10.99%
15	OTHER	100	13	13.00%
18	TOTAL	29,283	3,544	12.10%

Applying a 1-sided hypothesis test for equality of proportions between the sample of orange cars and non-orange cars in the testing partition yields a *p*-value of 0.109 (Equation 2).

> prop.test(c(14, 3530), c(162, 29121), alternative="less")$p.value(Eqn 2 in R code)

[1] 0.1087065

This *p*-value indicates that the proportion of bad buys among orange cars is low, but not low enough to be conclusive at the typical levels of significance. (In medical journals, for example, a significance of below 5% is required to publish.) In other words, we would hesitate to conclude that orange cars have a true proportion of bad buys lower than non-orange cars.

This result reveals the fragility of the original, seemingly confident finding, but is not a solution to the actual issues of what are the most interesting findings, and how unlikely they are. The *p*-value for the test dataset is much higher than we previously saw, primarily because the dataset is smaller. If another sample put a different percentage of cars in the testing sample, we'd come up with a different *p*-value. Partitioning tends to reduce significance since it's harder for a random finding to show up on both data sets. It's a step in the right direction for reducing the vast search effect.

Yet, even partitioning may not protect us unless we are careful. When we make a hypothesis using the training partition, evaluate that hypothesis on the test partition, and then return to training to revise that hypothesis or make new ones, we still run the risk of fooling ourselves. By alternating between training and testing, we've created an information "leak" from the future (testing) to the present (training), which can lead to erroneous conclusions. For this reason, data miners often split the data into three groups: training, validation, and testing. This allows them to employ some back-and-forth between the first two, while saving the test dataset for a single, final evaluation.

Solution 2: Mathematical Inference

We've established that the best way to determine if orange cars are really better buys is to gather brand new data and test our hypothesis on that data. However, when that is impractical, we noted that we could have used partitioning to both develop and test our hypothesis using the existing dataset. Since it may be too late for that, and single samples have a lot of variation, is there anything else we can do? Is there some way to account for the fact that we both developed and tested our hypothesis on the same dataset?

The following two approaches are attempts to do that. Each has limitations, but both are useful. The key to both of these solutions lies in the redefinition of our question. Previously, we ran a hypothesis test that answered the question, "How likely is it that the proportion of bad buys among orange cars would be so low by chance alone?" This led to a misleading result because orange was self-selected based on its own "interestingness."

A better question would be, "How likely is it that the proportion of bad buys among *some*-colored cars would be so unusual by chance alone?" This question is better because it compares the most interesting observed result (orange), not with what we would expect at random from orange, but with what we would expect at random from the *most interesting color* (whatever it may be). It assumes that we could have selected any one of the 15 different colors, and it accounts, at least in part, for how our hypothesis itself could have been different if the data were different.

You may have noticed that we used the term "most interesting," rather than "lowest proportion." The reason for this is two-fold: First, we should recognize that a color group having an especially *high* proportion of bad buys might also be interesting. We might want to know what color car to buy as well as what color to avoid, so we will consider both possibilities. Second, we use the term "interesting," because a low proportion, as shown in the Figures, does not take into account sample size. For example, if there were 3 neon cars in the dataset, and none were deemed bad buys, the sample proportion for the neon color would be 0%!

Obviously that would not convince us that neon cars are better buys than other colors. Our intuition would correctly tell us we don't have enough data. For this reason, a better measure of "most interesting" is lowest *p*-value. By considering sample size, *p*-values, provide a measure of how *unusually* high or low a proportion is. Therefore, what we want to determine is the probability that the lowest *p*-value for any color is at least as low as the observed *p*-value for orange, under the null (or default) hypothesis that it is truly all random.

Our first cut at this is through algebra. Orange's *p*-value of 0.00675 means that 0.675% of the time a group the size of orange would have a proportion that low by chance alone[36]. Additionally, it implies that 1.35%

---

36 Assuming that the true underlying proportion of bad buys among orange and non-orange cars is equal.

of the time (twice as often), orange would have a proportion that is that *extreme* (low or high) by chance alone. Furthermore, because sample size is accounted for, it implies that 0.675% of the time, red would have a proportion that is unusually low; and that 1.35% of the time, red would have a proportion that is unusually extreme, by chance alone. Given that this holds for every color, and that there are a total of 15 colors, we can estimate the probability that *no* color would have a result as interesting as orange did by calculating the probability of "not orange" *and* "not blue" *and* "not gold" *and* "not green" and so on. In probability, "and" means multiply, and "not orange" means "1 – orange." Therefore, we can calculate the probability of "not any color" as follows:

Number of colors = 15

2-sided (as extreme as): $P = (1 - 0.0135)^{15} = 0.816$

1-sided (as low as): $P = (1 - 0.00675)^{15} = 0.903$

This means that 81.6% of the time, no color would have a result as extreme as the result we actually observed in orange. Conversely, it means that 18.4% of the time some color would have a similarly extreme result. This suggests that our result for orange is somewhat unusual, but not that unusual. Certainly it is much less unusual than our original *p*-value suggested.

Additionally, even if we apply a 1-sided test and only consider unusually low (not high) proportions, our calculations suggest that we should still expect to find a proportion at least as unusually low as that of orange 9.7% of the time. Therefore, a *p*-value of 0.097 or 0.184 would be a much better indicator of true significance than 0.00675.

Solution 3: Simulation – Target Shuffling

Another way to answer the question "How likely is it that the proportion of bad buys among *some*-colored cars would be that unusual by chance alone?" is to apply a technique called "target shuffling" (invented, or more accurately, rediscovered by one of us). This technique is a form of simulation in which we essentially repeat our experiment many times to simulate the results one might expect at random. Its name comes from our randomly "shuffling[37]" the values of the target (dependent) variable, while leaving the rest of the dataset in place. This is illustrated for a small sample of data in Figure 5.

---

37 Shuffling denotes random reordering or sampling without replacement.

Input	Target		Input	Target
Color	**Bad Buy**		**Color**	**Bad Buy**
BLACK	TRUE		BLACK	FALSE
BEIGE	FALSE		BEIGE	FALSE
BLACK	FALSE		BLACK	FALSE
MAROON	FALSE		MAROON	FALSE
GREY	TRUE		GREY	FALSE
GREEN	FALSE		GREEN	TRUE
YELLOW	FALSE		YELLOW	FALSE
BLUE	FALSE	Shuffle	BLUE	FALSE
BLACK	FALSE		BLACK	FALSE
GREEN	FALSE		GREEN	FALSE
GREEN	FALSE		GREEN	FALSE
PURPLE	FALSE		PURPLE	TRUE
BEIGE	FALSE		BEIGE	TRUE
GOLD	FALSE		GOLD	FALSE
RED	FALSE		RED	FALSE
YELLOW	FALSE		YELLOW	FALSE
RED	FALSE		RED	FALSE
BROWN	TRUE		BROWN	FALSE

Figure 5: Example of Target Shuffling

Target shuffling creates a dataset in which we *know* that no real relationship exists between the target variable and any input variable. It creates a world in which the null hypothesis holds. It is to this shuffled dataset that we apply our new hypothesis, model, or modeling process[38]. Then we measure the new significance of our hypothesis or performance of the model. By repeating this process many times, we are able to create a distribution of "performances" that we know are attributable to random chance alone. Therefore, we are able to compare our best results on real data to our "best" results on random data (called "Best Apparent Discoveries" or BADs) to get a better sense of just how significant our original results are.

This technique has great value for at least three reasons. First, with today's computing power it is often much faster and easier to simulate results than to go through the sometimes painstaking effort of estimating them mathematically. Second, this technique is much more intuitive to a non-statistician, and therefore the results are accepted as credible by those who do not understand the underlying statistics. Third, since everyone occasionally makes mistakes, this technique is a great way to confirm and double-check a result that has been calculated statistically.

38 Applying a modeling process would entail retraining the model on the shuffled data and is an effective method of testing for overfit.

In order to apply target shuffling to our problem, we followed this process.

1. Shuffle the vector of bad buys (containing 8,951 true values and 63,930 false values)
2. Aggregate to get bad-buy count by color
3. Calculate an equality of proportions hypothesis test for each color vs. all other colors
4. Determine the minimum p-value across all colors
5. Repeat this process 10,000 times

When running a 2-sided hypothesis test, and thereby testing for extreme proportions (whether high or low), we found the distribution of Figure 6, in which 1,635 out of the 10,000 trials (16.4%) yielded a minimum p-value of less than or equal to our threshold value of 0.0135.

Minimum P-values (2-sided test shuffled)

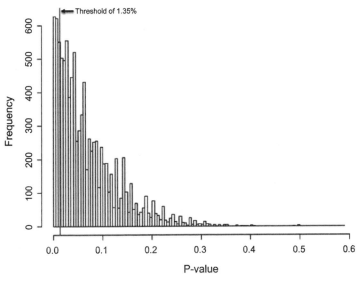

Figure 6

This would indicate that we could expect *some*-colored car to achieve a result as extreme as orange's roughly 16.4% of the time if no difference in proportion between car colors truly exists. As before, we also ran a 1-sided hypothesis test to test for low proportions only, and found that 715 out of 10,000 trials (7.2%) yielded a minimum p-value of less than or equal to our threshold value of 0.00675 (Figure 7).

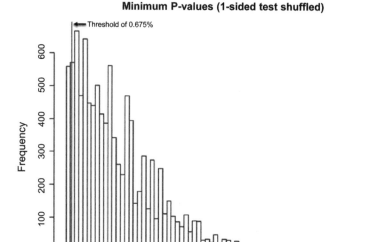

Figure 7

This tells us that we could expect some-colored car to achieve a result as unusually low as orange's roughly 7.2% of the time if no actual difference in proportion between car colors exists.

Now, for the curious reader, there are a few subtleties to observe. First, to construct each dummy target vector we have used "shuffling" rather than "re-sampling." In other words, we have used sampling *without* replacement, rather than sampling *with* replacement. Shuffling has the advantage of limiting the sources of variation by keeping the overall bad-buy proportion constant. However, it also introduces a slight dependence between the proportion of bad buys for any given color and the proportion of bad buys among all other colors[39]. Therefore, we tried repeating our experiment using sampling with replacement to test the strength of this. We achieved simulated *p*-values of 0.1624 and 0.0721, respectively, which nearly match our previous values of 0.1635 and 0.0715. The type of sampling used is a minor factor.

The second subtlety involves the difference between our simulated *p*-values of 0.1635 and 0.0715 and our approximate algebraic *p*-values of

---

39 This is because if the total number of bad buys is t and the number of bad buys for a given color is n, then the number of bad buys for all other colors must be $t - n$.

0.184 and 0.097. A major reason for this becomes clear when we look at the distribution of all *p*-values for all colors over the 10,000 iterations with replacement[40] as in Figure 8.

P-values for 2-sided Test with Replacement

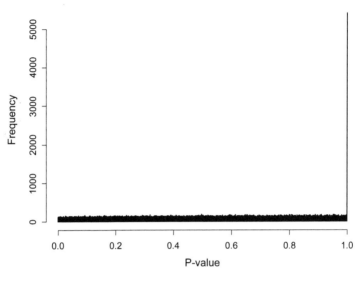

Figure 8

Note that there is a major spike at $p = 1$. That's because we are working with whole numbers and the distribution of sample proportions is non-continuous. Analogously, if we ran a binomial hypothesis test to test whether a coin is fair with 5 trials, the only possible resulting *p*-values would be 0.0625, 0.375, and 1, as shown in Table 5.

Table 5: p-values for Coin with 5 Flips

Heads	Pct	P-value
0	3.1%	0.0625
1	15.6%	0.375
2	31.3%	1
3	31.3%	1
4	15.6%	0.375
5	3.1%	0.0625

---

40 The distribution for trials with replacement (rather than without) is shown because the distribution is cleaner and illustrates the point more clearly.

In the coin experiment of Table 5, 6.25% of the time the outcome is either all heads or no heads, and the *p*-value for *each* of those cases is 0.0625. Thus, 6.25% of the time the *p*-value is <= 0.0625. Likewise, 37.5% of the time the *p*-value is less than or equal to 0.375. Yet, it is not true that 50% of the time the *p*-value is less than or equal to 0.5. Rather, that is the case only 37.5% of the time! *P*-values of 1 are very common.

Combining many such distributions together (as happens with multiple bins such as color) produces distributions like Figure 8, in which there is a piling up of values at 1. Also, the proportion of *p*-values less than or equal to a given value are actually not equal to the value itself, as one might theoretically expect.

For example, the true proportion of *p*-values that were less than or equal to 0.5 was only 47.8%, rather than 50% as expected; and the true proportion of *p*-values that were less than 0.0135 was only 0.01207[41]. This explains why our simulated *p*-value is a bit less than the one we calculated. It illustrates the value of simulation, as effects like this are very hard to anticipate!

There is More to Discover...

Before drawing any conclusions, note that the hypothesis test for equality of proportions is not limited to comparing only two samples. In fact, it can compare *n*-samples, which means that it can provide the probability that the total variation between them would be as great if all were drawn randomly from populations with matching proportions. Therefore, we can easily test the hypothesis that the proportion of bad buys among all colors of cars is the same.

```
> prop.test(c(1843, 1506, 1189, 911, 858, 825, 737, 402, 260, 211, 56, 34, 56, 34, 29),
+ c(14875, 12123, 10347, 7887, 7627, 6257, 5231, 3194, 2046, 1584, 436, 415, 373, 244, 242),
+ alternative="two.sided")$p.value
[1] 5.149562e-06
```

Surprisingly, this test results in a *p*-value of 0.00000515! In other words, the test suggests that there is almost no chance that the variation in bad-buy

---

41 Not coincidentally, note that $1 - (1 - 0.01207)^{15} = 16.7\%$, which is much closer to our simulated *p*-value of 16.2%.

proportion by car color is the result of random variation alone. To understand why this would be, let us look more closely. Notice the p-values we obtain if we apply a two-sided test for equality of proportions between each color and all other colors in the original dataset (Table 6).

Table 6: P-values for Proportion of Bad across all Colors (Looking for either High or Low)

Color	Count	Bad Buys	Percent	P-value
SILVER	14875	1843	12.39%	0.6622
WHITE	12123	1506	12.42%	0.61504
BLUE	10347	1189	11.49%	0.00858
GREY	7887	911	11.55%	0.03786
BLACK	7627	858	11.25%	0.00393
RED	6257	825	13.19%	0.02398
GOLD	5231	737	14.09%	0.00004
GREEN	3194	402	12.59%	0.6111
MAROON	2046	260	12.71%	0.57452
BEIGE	1584	211	13.32%	0.21678
BROWN	436	56	12.84%	0.77514
ORANGE	415	34	8.19%	0.01351
PURPLE	373	56	15.01%	0.12541
YELLOW	244	34	13.93%	0.49007
OTHER	242	29	11.98%	0.96532
TOTAL	72881	8951	12.28%	

As before, we see that orange has a p-value of 0.0135. Yet, surprisingly, this is the 4th lowest (most interesting) p-value! In fact, the p-value for gold is over 300 times as significant as that of orange! No color has a proportion as different from the mean as orange does, but when we account for sample size, we find that the observed proportions for blue, black, and gold are all more *unusually* extreme than that of orange. In fact, the proportion for gold appears to be so unusually high that, even with the vast search effect, it would appear highly improbable to have occurred by chance.

What does this mean? Are we to conclude that gold cars are bad buys? First, note that statistical significance does not necessarily correspond to practical significance. The observed proportion of bad buys among gold cars is 14.1%, which is only 2% higher than the observed proportion in non-gold cars (12.1%). This might be useful information, but it is less useful than knowing that the true proportion of bad buys among orange cars is actually about 4% lower than that of non-orange cars.

Second, we recognize that it is possible that this difference in proportion is attributable to some sampling bias or correlated factor and not to car color, per se. For example, perhaps bad-buy proportion varies with the age of the vehicle, or perhaps car color preferences tend to vary with time. Nevertheless, it seems convincing that there is *something* non-random in the relationship between car color (especially gold) and bad-buy proportion, and it would likely be worth further investigation to find the reason(s).

Conclusions

Note that the truly interesting result (gold) was not identified originally, but orange was identified due to the visualization we employed (Figure 1). The visualization was entirely appropriate and accurate, but it was susceptible to the small-sample effect, so it led us astray. Only by testing using *p*-values, which take into account the sample size, did we learn that there were three colors more statistically interesting than the visual outlier color orange.

Then we learned not to stop at the *p*-values, or trust them as indicators of likelihood, since we didn't approach the data with well-formed hypotheses to test, which is what *p*-values were designed for. It is best to estimate the probability that *some*-colored cars would have a proportion as unusual as was observed in orange. We tried both mathematical inference and simulation (target shuffling), and checked for unusually low proportions and for extreme proportions, either low or high. Our results are in Table 7.

Table 7: Summary of 1-Tailed (as Low as) and 2-Tailed (as Extreme as) Tests by Two Methods

	As Low As	As Extreme As
Math	0.097	0.184
Target Shuffling	0.072	0.164

We believe the most realistic probability result for assessing the true interestingness of orange is revealed by target shuffling, with an extreme of 16.4%. It measures the probability of *some* color obtaining a proportion at least as extreme as was observed for orange, if the underlying reality is that there is no relationship with color. We may still find this worth acting on, or testing on new data, but the finding is by no means as unusual as we first suspected visually, or even after using our first statistical test (0.675%)!

Still, based on the equality of proportions test on all colors, it is highly likely that there is some relationship between car color and bad-buy proportion (*p*-value of 0.00000515). Using *p*-values to account for sample sizes, three other colors were identified as statistically more interesting than orange. Further investigation would be required to reveal whether color is fate, or whether color is really confounded with a more meaningful variable. It is often true that if the relationship holds up out-of-sample, it will be worth acting on, whether or not we are satisfied with an explanation!

ABOUT THE AUTHORS

Jeff Deal is the Vice President of Operations for Elder Research. Working out of the firm's corporate headquarters in Charlottesville, Virginia, he oversees operational, contractual, and financial matters. Drawing on his more than twenty-five years of management experience in business and government, he regularly helps organizational clients clarify and attain their data analytics goals.

A frequent speaker on the subject of organizational challenges to meeting data analytics goals, Mr. Deal is the program chair for the annual *Predictive Analytics World – Healthcare* conference, which annually attracts leading analytics professionals in the healthcare industry from around the country. He holds a Master of Health Administration degree from Virginia Commonwealth University in Richmond, Virginia, and a Bachelor of Arts degree from the College of William and Mary in Williamsburg, Virginia, where he was a member of the wrestling team. Jeff and his wife, Jennifer, have four children. In his spare time he enjoys hiking, reading, and an increasing amount of recreational travel with his wife, now that their kids have all moved out of the house.

Gerhard Pilcher, Chief Executive Officer for Elder Research, is responsible for the firm's northern Virginia office. He has more than thirty years of industry and consulting experience with commercial businesses and government institutions in the United States and abroad. His specialties include fraud detection, financial risk management, and healthcare outcomes.

Mr. Pilcher earned a Master of Science degree in analytics from the Institute for Advanced Analytics at North Carolina State University in Raleigh, North Carolina. He is an adjunct faculty member in the math and statistics masters degree program at Georgetown University, and a regular instructor at the SAS Business Knowledge Series course, "Data Mining: Principles and Best Practices." Gerhard currently serves on the advisory boards of the Institute for Advanced Analytics and the Masters in Science in Business Analytics program at George Washington University.

Gerhard and his wife, Denise, have two children. In his spare time, he especially enjoys outdoor activities, including mountaineering and trail running.

ABOUT ELDER RESEARCH, INC.

Elder Research, Inc. is a recognized industry leader in the science, practice, and technology of advanced analytics, with vast experience in data transformation and model construction. Founded in 1995 by Dr. John Elder, the company has helped many government agencies and Fortune Global 500 companies solve real-world problems in diverse industry segments.

Elder Research's areas of expertise include data science, text mining, data visualization, scientific software engineering, and technical teaching. By combining the business domain expertise of its clients with its own deep understanding of advanced analytics, the firm creates teams that can extract actionable value from data and transform data, domain knowledge, and algorithmic innovations into world-class analytic solutions.

Corporate Headquarters:
300 West Main Street, Suite 301
Charlottesville, VA 22903
434.973.7673

Additional Offices:

Washington, DC
2101 Wilson Blvd., Suite 900
Arlington, VA 22201

Raleigh, NC
14E Peace Street
Raleigh, NC 27604

Baltimore, MD
839 Elkridge Landing, Suite 215
Linthicum, MD 21090

INDEX

Note: Page numbers in *italics* refer to charts or graphs.

humility, 42–43

Hux, Dustin, 48

hypothesis statements, 130–34, 135–37, 139–145, 146, 148

I

IBM
  Datastage, 49, 50
  Modeler, 54
  SPSS, 50, 51, 52
  Watson, 3, 3n2, 112

ICDM (IEEE Conference on Data Mining), 64

IEEE Conference on Data Mining (ICDM), 64

IHS Global Insight, 39

illustrative models, building, 90–92

implementation of recommendations, 25–26, 27–29, 30

inconsistency in the data, 50, 82–83

inductive techniques of data mining, 7, 12–13, 99–100

information, growth in, 2, 5

information technology specialists, 37, 126

in-house analytics programs, 59

initial projects, 23–24, 33

innovation, 125, 128

Institute of Advanced Analytics at North Carolina State University, 40

integer programming, 11

Internal Revenue Service (IRS), xviii

Internet, 2, 2–3

interpretability/accuracy trade-off, 98, 102

J

jackknifing, 107

Java, 49

JMP, 50

Jones, Bryan
  and data access, 84
  and deployment of model, 122
  and hiring consultants, 61
  leadership role of, 29
  and model building, 96
  and staffing data analytics projects, 39
  and tool acquisition, 53
  and transformation of organization, 127, 128
  and understanding the business, 75
  and validating the model, 111

JRules, 10

K

KDD (Knowledge Discovery and Data Mining), 64

KDnuggets, 36

KETL, 49, 50

K-means clustering, 10

Knime, 52, 54

knowledge, sources of, 19

Knowledge Discovery and Data Mining (KDD), 64

Kuri, 51

KXEN, 54

L

leading data analytics initiatives, 21–33
  and business objectives, xx
  and commitment of organization, 25, 30
  and defining focus, 24–25
  and expectations management, 26–27
  and implementation of recommendations, 25–26, 27–29